Disney's Kim Possible

VOLUME 7

SERIES CREATED BY
BOB SCHOOLEY AND MARK McCORKLE

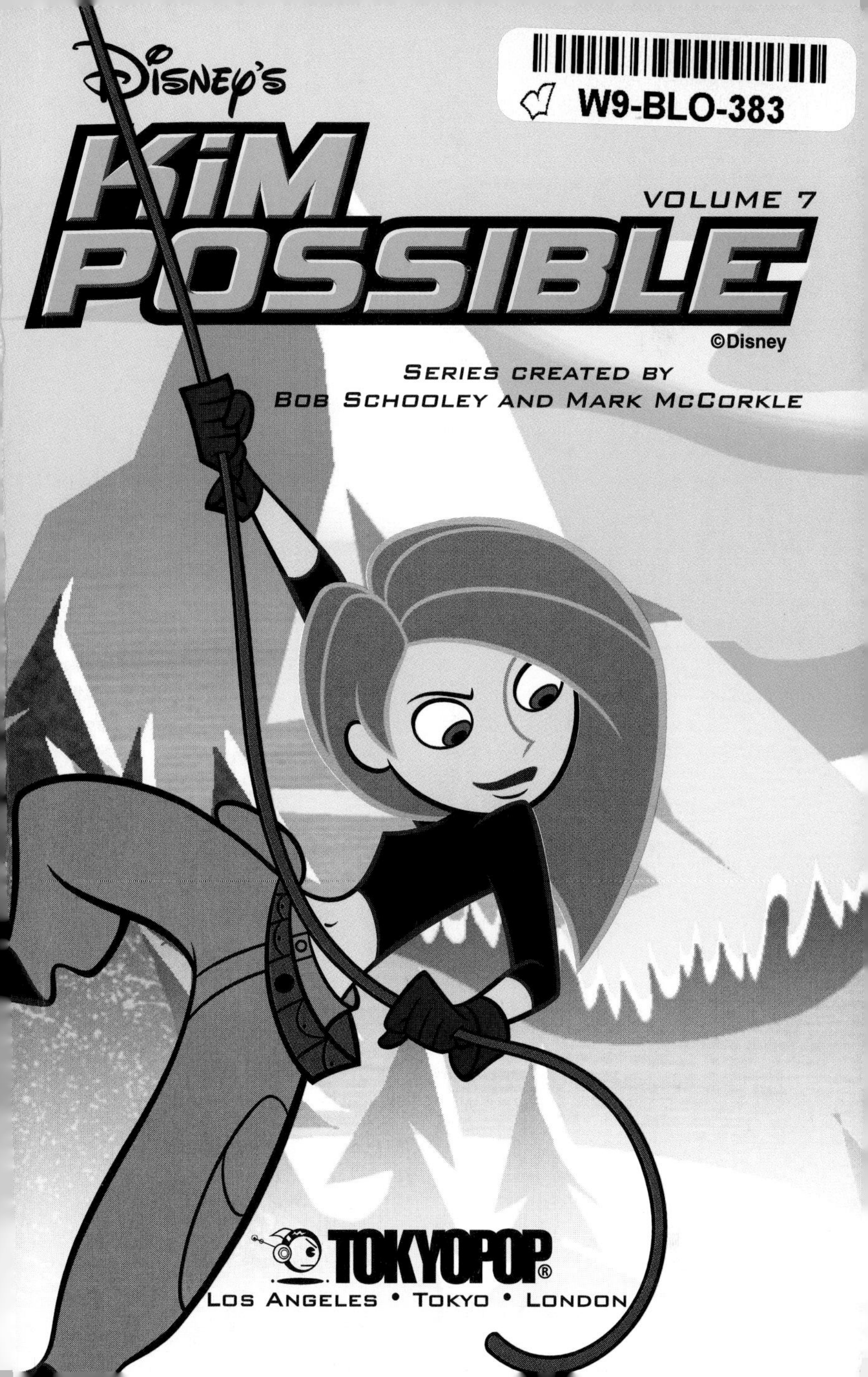

TOKYOPOP®
LOS ANGELES • TOKYO • LONDON

Contributing Editors - Ivy Garcia, Amy Court Kaemon & Paul Morrissey
Graphic Design & Lettering - Jennifer Nunn-Iwai
Graphic Artist - Tomás Montalvo-Lagos
Cover Layout - Patrick Hook

Editor - Elizabeth Hurchalla, Jod Kaftan & Erin Stein
Managing Editor - Jill Freshney
Production Coordinator - Antonio DePietro
Production Manager - Jennifer Miller
Art Director - Matt Alford
Editorial Director - Jeremy Ross
VP of Production - Ron Klamert
President & C.O.O. - John Parker
Publisher & C.E.O. - Stuart Levy

Come visit us online at www.TOKYOPOP.com

A **TOKYOPOP**® Cine-Manga™
TOKYOPOP Inc.
5900 Wilshire Blvd., Suite 2000, Los Angeles, CA 90036

Kim Possible Volume 7
© 2004 Disney Enterprises, Inc.

ISBN: 1-59182-570-9
First TOKYOPOP printing: July 2004

10 9 8 7 6 5 4 3 2 1

Printed in Canada

DISNEY's

KiM POSSIBLE

VOLUME 7

©Disney

CONTENTS:

CRUSH...6
MONKEY NINJAS IN SPACE..............48

CHARACTER BIOS

KIM POSSIBLE

A STUDENT AT MIDDLETON HIGH SCHOOL WHO LOVES CHEERLEADING, SHOPPING AND HANGING OUT WITH HER BEST FRIEND, RON. BUT KIM'S NO ORDINARY GIRL—SHE CAN DO ANYTHING, INCLUDING SAVING THE WORLD IN HER SPARE TIME.

RON STOPPABLE

KIM'S BEST FRIEND AND SIDEKICK.

RUFUS

RON'S PET NAKED MOLE RAT.

WADE

THE 10-YEAR-OLD GENIUS WHO RUNS KIM'S WEBSITE AND KEEPS HER UPDATED ON EVIL-SCHEME DEVELOPMENTS.

KIM'S MOM

A BRAIN SURGEON.

KIM'S DAD

A ROCKET SCIENTIST.

JOSH MANKEY

THE CUTEST BOY IN SCHOOL.

DRAKKEN

A BAD GUY WHO WANTS TO TAKE OVER
THE WORLD.

SHEGO

DRAKKEN'S GLAMOROUS HENCHGIRL.

LORD MONTY
FISKE/MONKEY FIST

A KUNG FU MASTER WHO CRAVES
ULTIMATE MONKEY POWERS.

FREDERICK

A MONKEY ASTRONAUT.

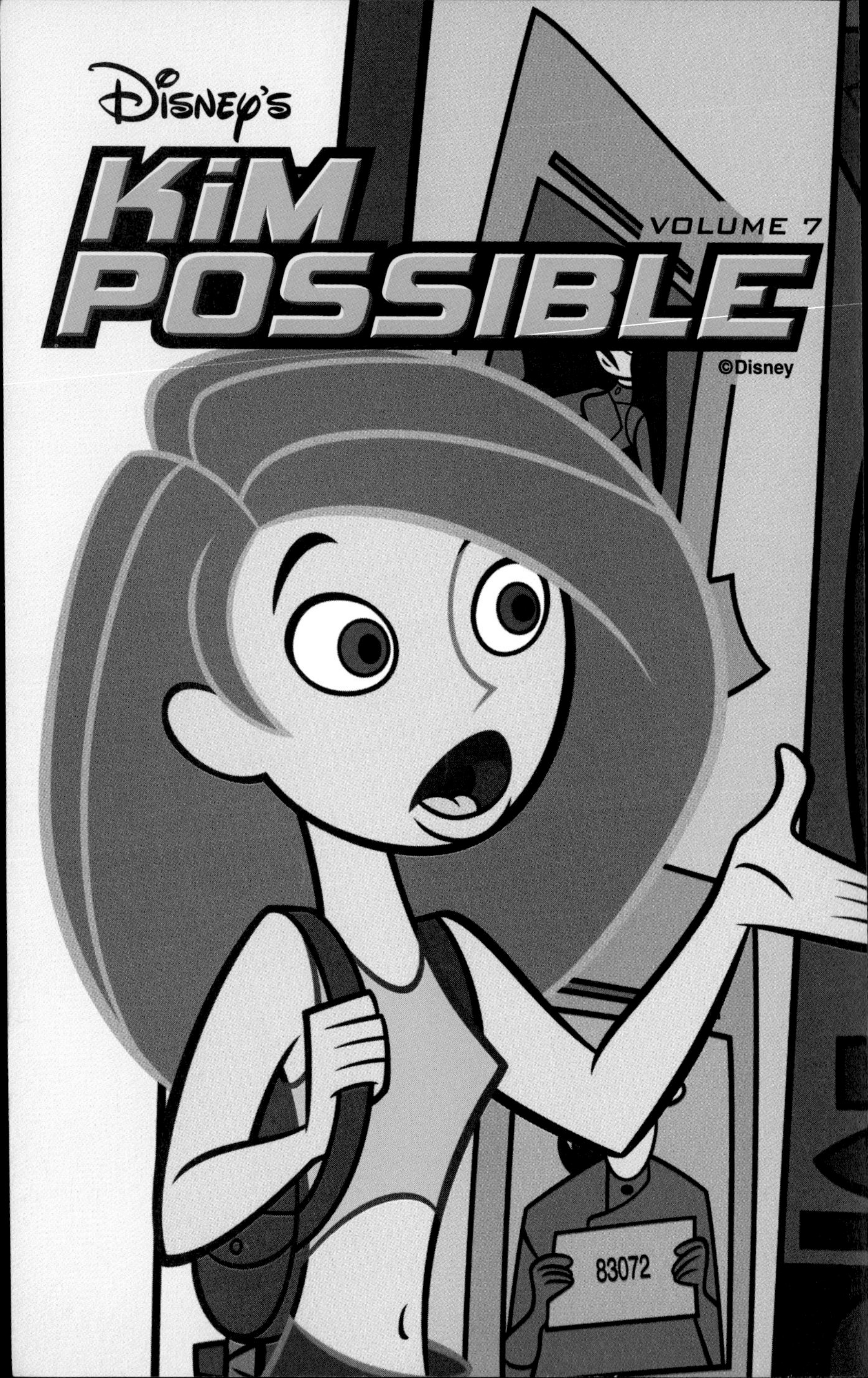
DISNEY'S
KIM POSSIBLE
VOLUME 7
©Disney
83072

Episode 13: Crush

Kim's crushing on the cutest boy in school. Will she be able to save a Japanese factory from Drakken's evil scheme and figure out how to ask Josh Mankey to the school dance?

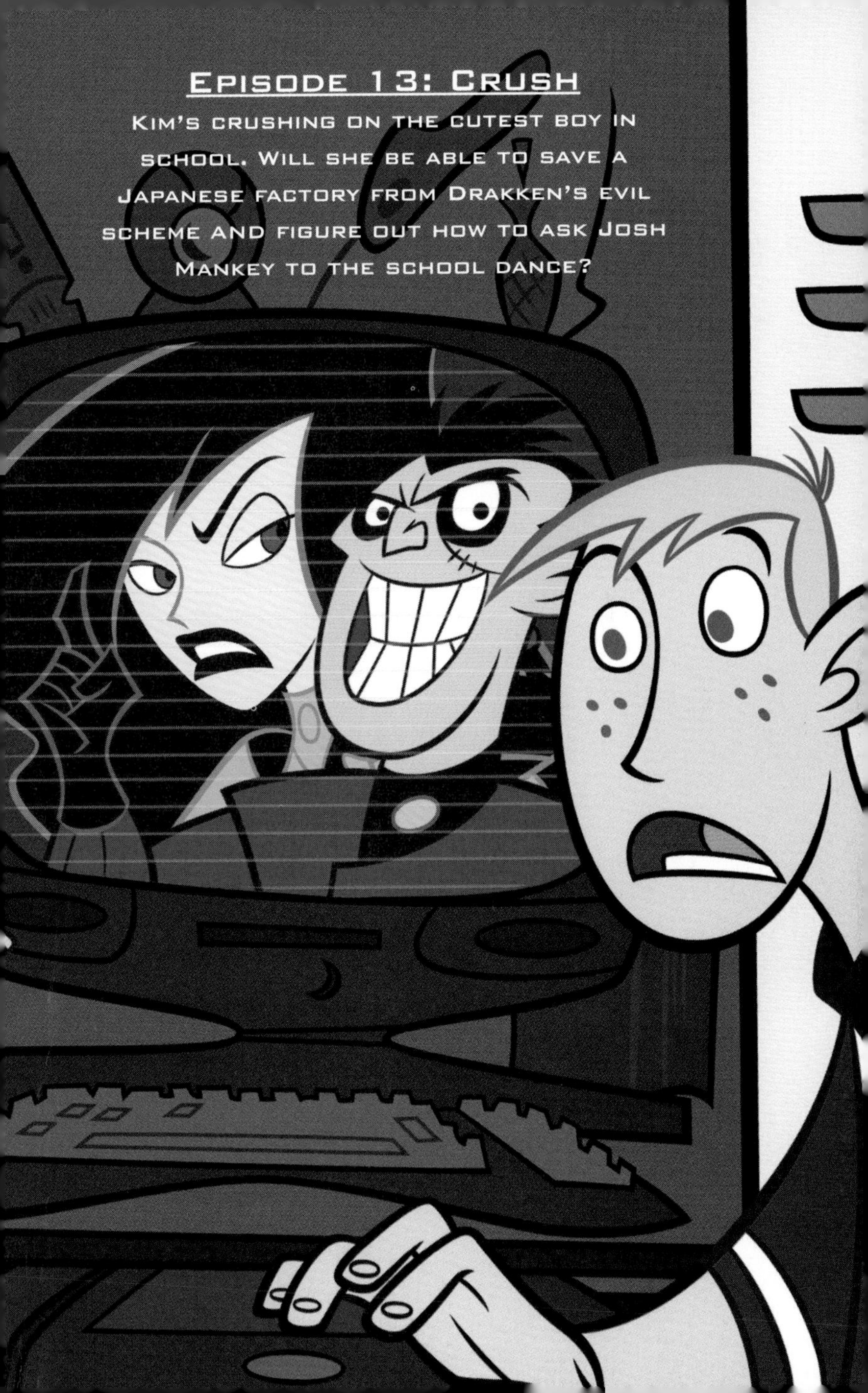

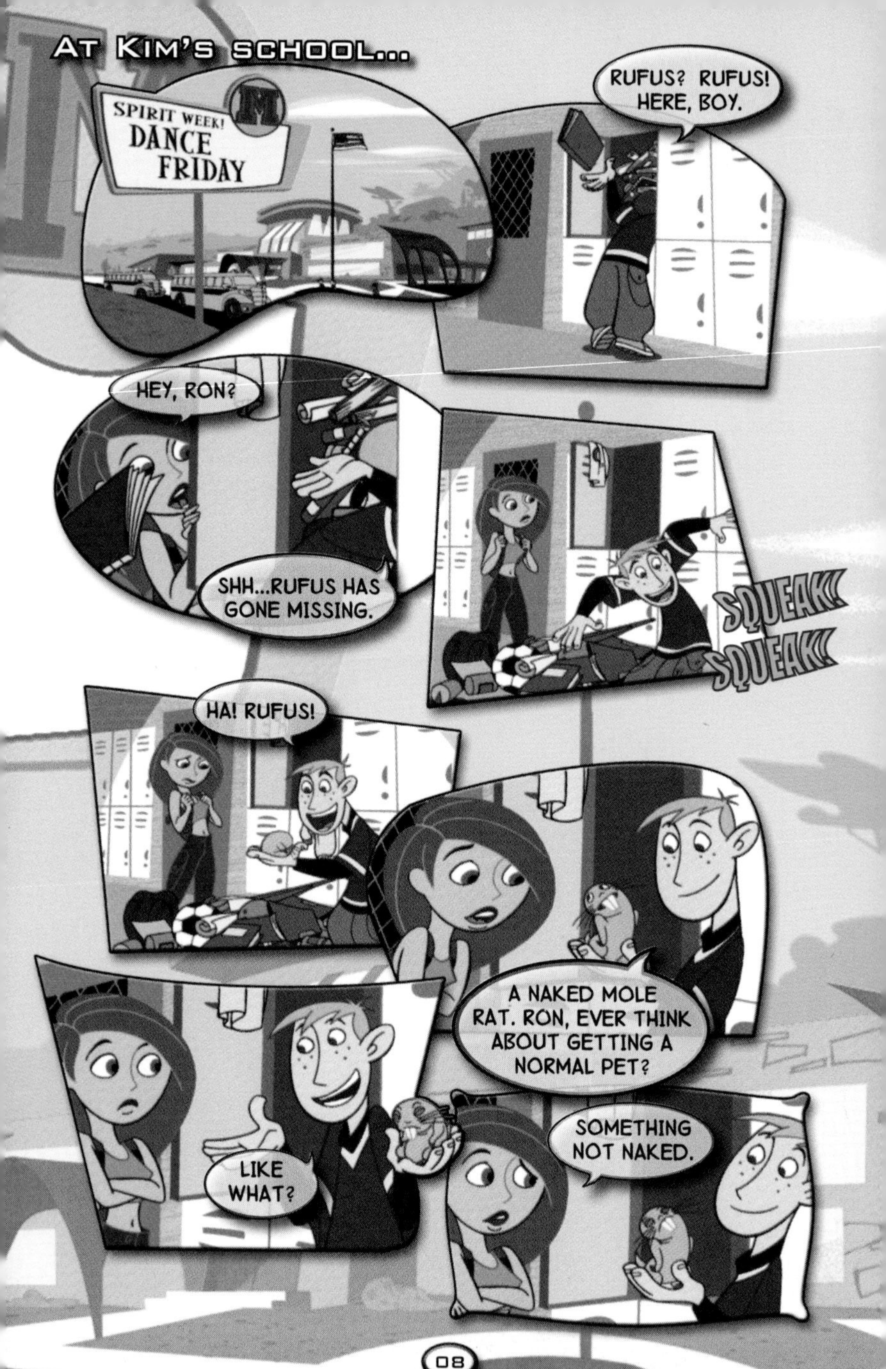
AT KIM'S SCHOOL...
SPIRIT WEEK!
DANCE
FRIDAY
RUFUS? RUFUS! HERE, BOY.
HEY, RON?
SHH...RUFUS HAS GONE MISSING.
SQUEAK!
SQUEAK!
HA! RUFUS!
A NAKED MOLE RAT. RON, EVER THINK ABOUT GETTING A NORMAL PET?
LIKE WHAT?
SOMETHING NOT NAKED.

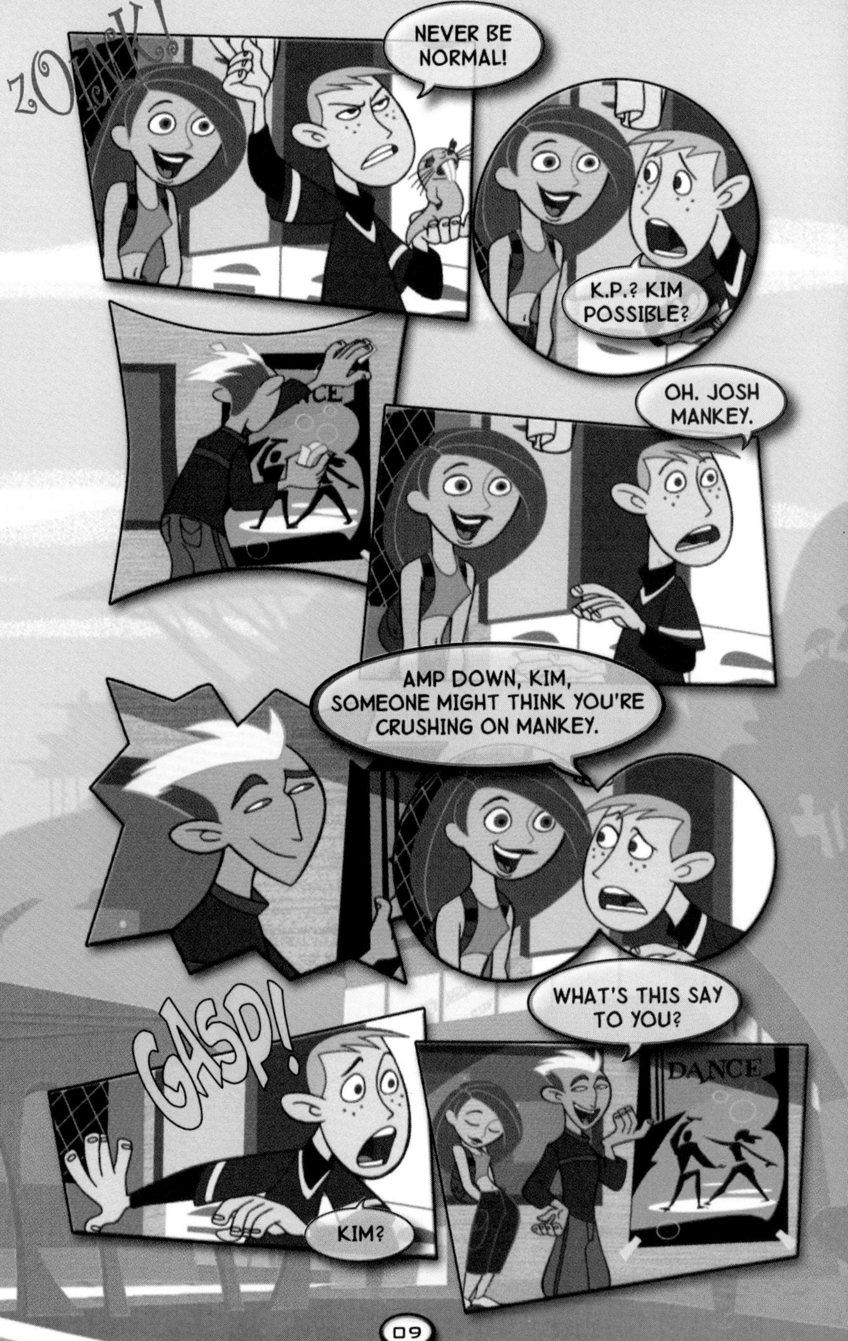
ZONK!
NEVER BE NORMAL!
K.P.? KIM POSSIBLE?
DANCE
OH. JOSH MANKEY.
AMP DOWN, KIM, SOMEONE MIGHT THINK YOU'RE CRUSHING ON MANKEY.
GASP!
WHAT'S THIS SAY TO YOU?
DANCE
KIM?

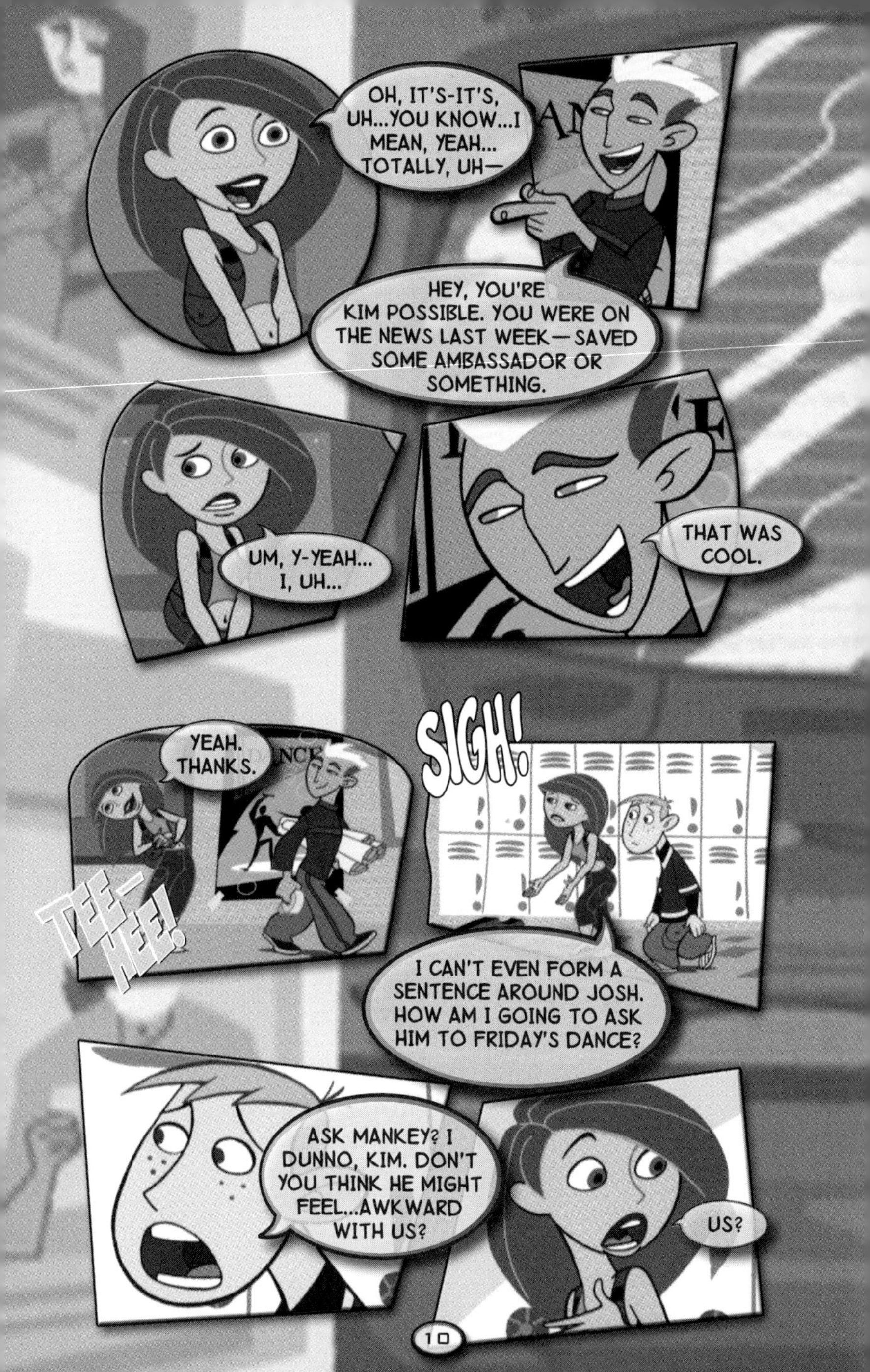

OH, IT'S-IT'S, UH...YOU KNOW...I MEAN, YEAH... TOTALLY, UH—
HEY, YOU'RE KIM POSSIBLE. YOU WERE ON THE NEWS LAST WEEK—SAVED SOME AMBASSADOR OR SOMETHING.
UM, Y-YEAH... I, UH...
THAT WAS COOL.
YEAH. THANKS.
TEE-HEE!
SIGH!
I CAN'T EVEN FORM A SENTENCE AROUND JOSH. HOW AM I GOING TO ASK HIM TO FRIDAY'S DANCE?
ASK MANKEY? I DUNNO, KIM. DON'T YOU THINK HE MIGHT FEEL...AWKWARD WITH US?
US?

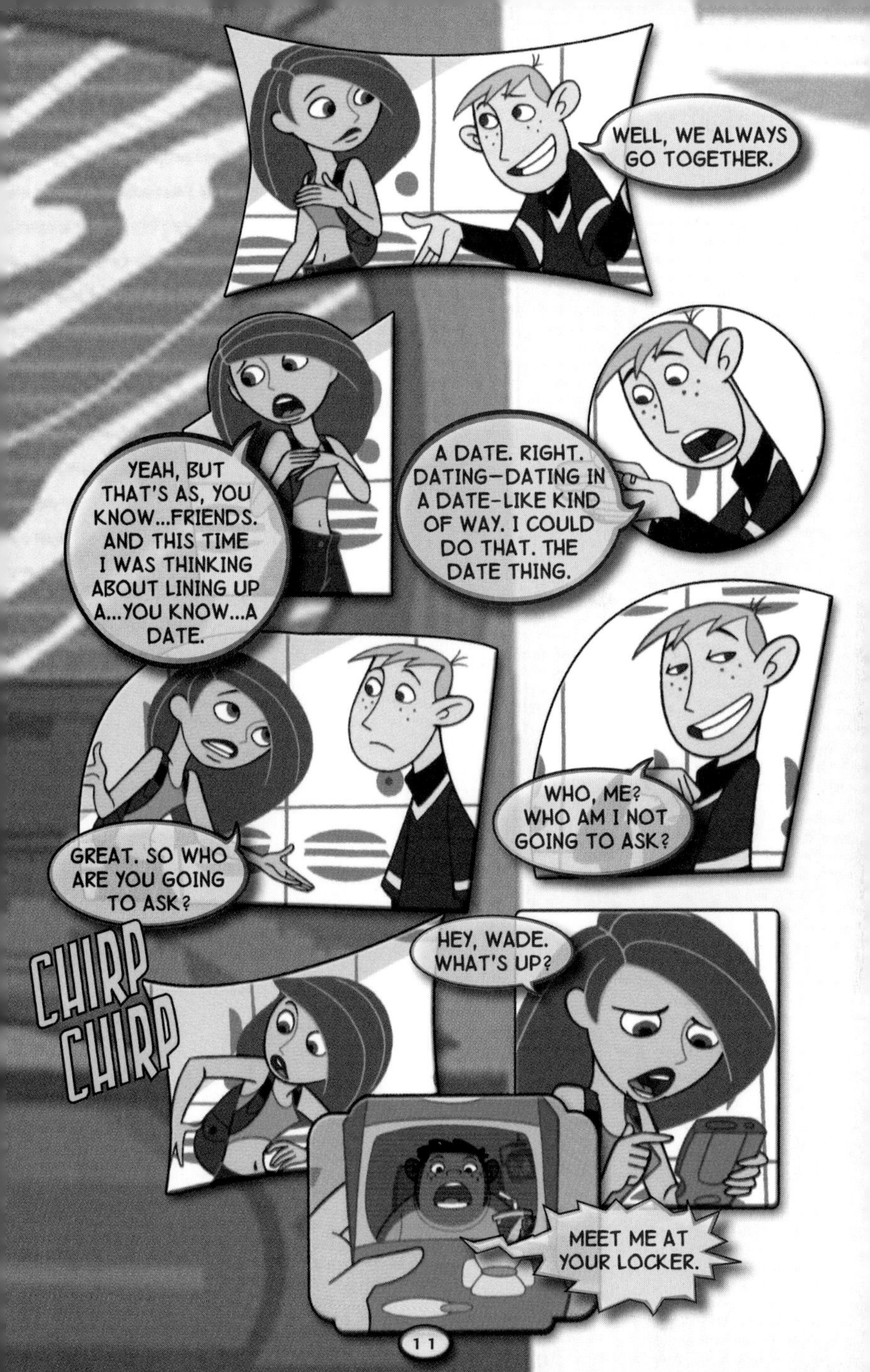
WELL, WE ALWAYS GO TOGETHER.
YEAH, BUT THAT'S AS, YOU KNOW...FRIENDS. AND THIS TIME I WAS THINKING ABOUT LINING UP A...YOU KNOW...A DATE.
A DATE. RIGHT. DATING—DATING IN A DATE-LIKE KIND OF WAY. I COULD DO THAT. THE DATE THING.
GREAT. SO WHO ARE YOU GOING TO ASK?
WHO, ME? WHO AM I NOT GOING TO ASK?
CHIRP CHIRP
HEY, WADE. WHAT'S UP?
MEET ME AT YOUR LOCKER.

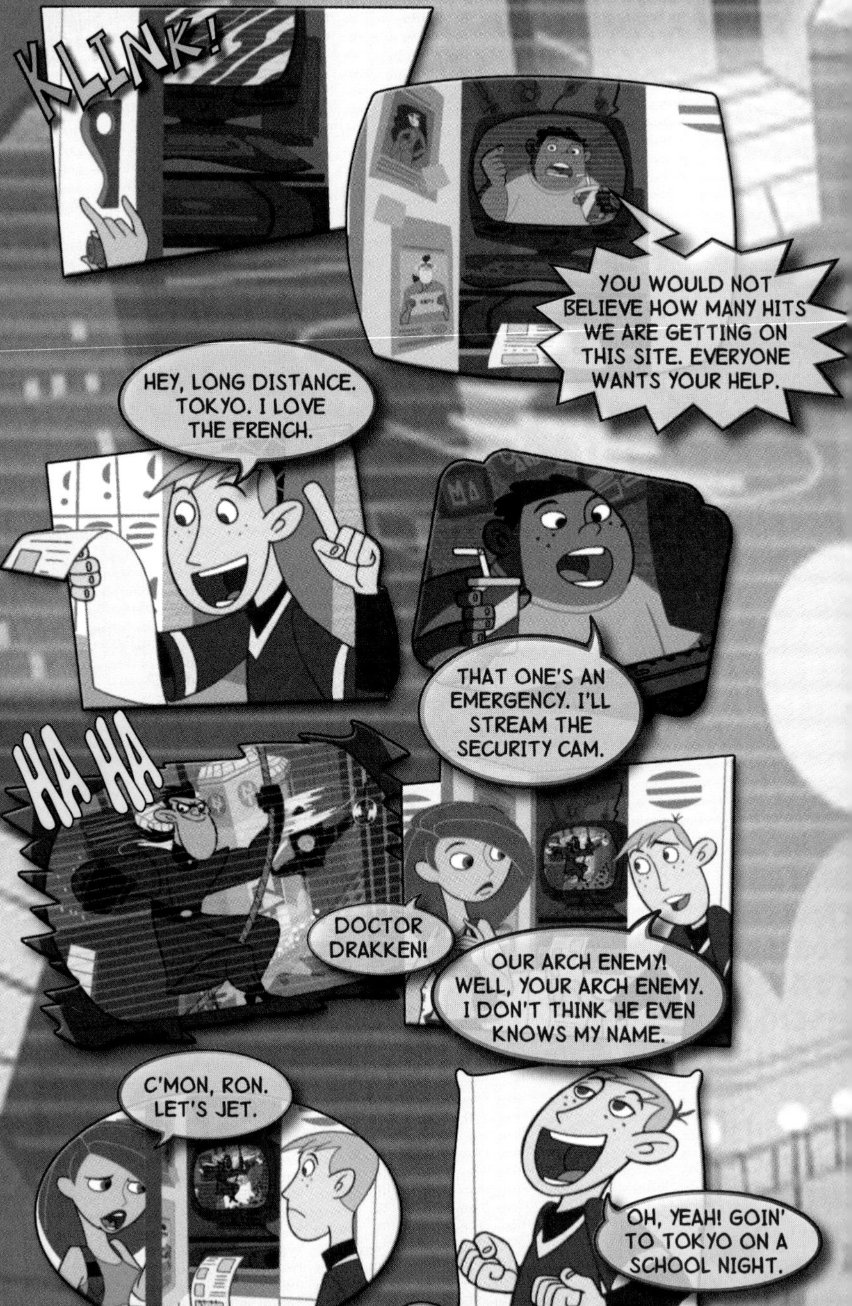
KLINK!
YOU WOULD NOT BELIEVE HOW MANY HITS WE ARE GETTING ON THIS SITE. EVERYONE WANTS YOUR HELP.
HEY, LONG DISTANCE. TOKYO. I LOVE THE FRENCH.
THAT ONE'S AN EMERGENCY. I'LL STREAM THE SECURITY CAM.
HA HA
DOCTOR DRAKKEN!
OUR ARCH ENEMY! WELL, YOUR ARCH ENEMY. I DON'T THINK HE EVEN KNOWS MY NAME.
C'MON, RON. LET'S JET.
OH, YEAH! GOIN' TO TOKYO ON A SCHOOL NIGHT.

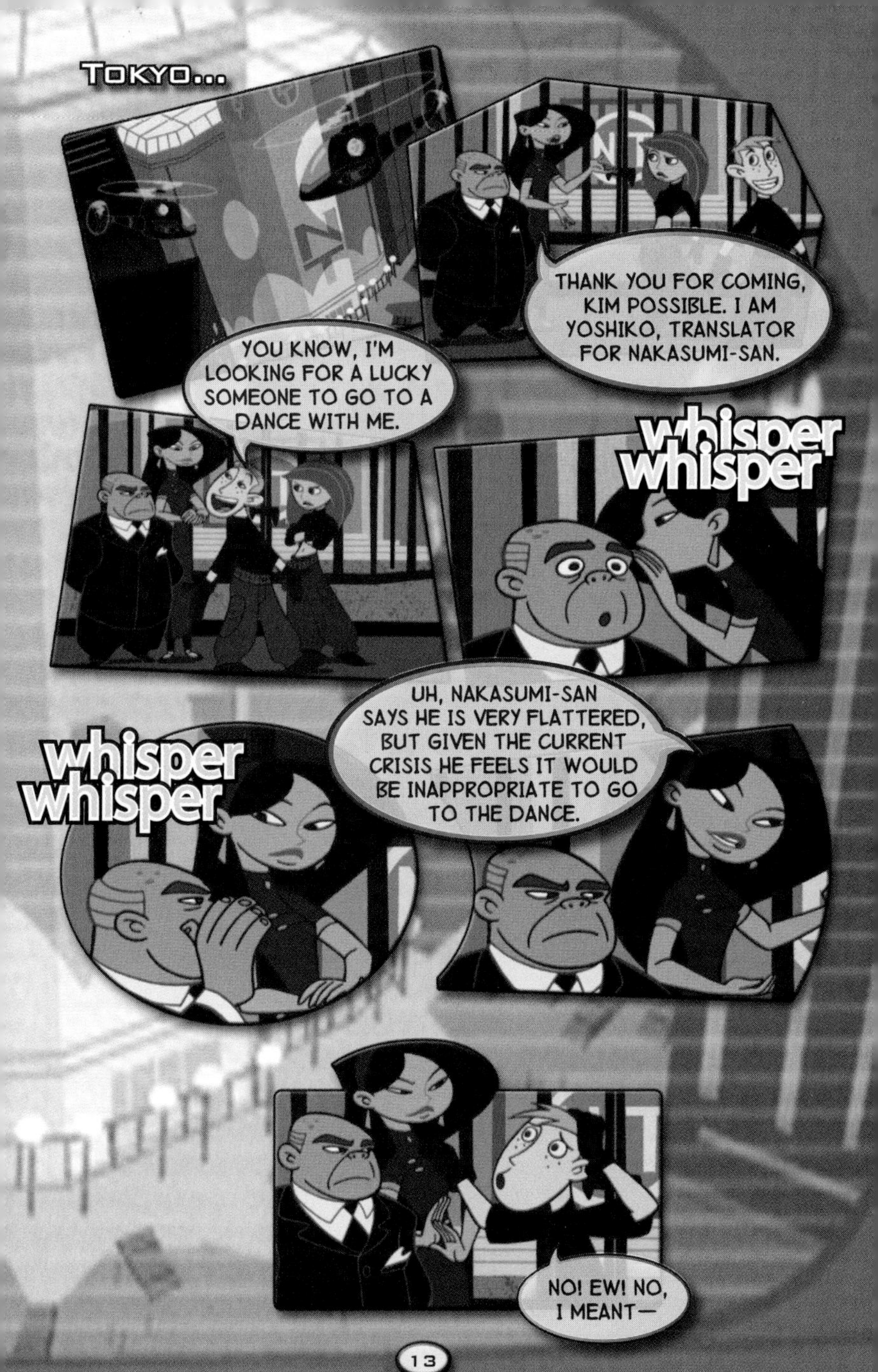
TOKYO...
THANK YOU FOR COMING, KIM POSSIBLE. I AM YOSHIKO, TRANSLATOR FOR NAKASUMI-SAN.
YOU KNOW, I'M LOOKING FOR A LUCKY SOMEONE TO GO TO A DANCE WITH ME.
whisper whisper
whisper whisper
UH, NAKASUMI-SAN SAYS HE IS VERY FLATTERED, BUT GIVEN THE CURRENT CRISIS HE FEELS IT WOULD BE INAPPROPRIATE TO GO TO THE DANCE.
NO! EW! NO, I MEANT—

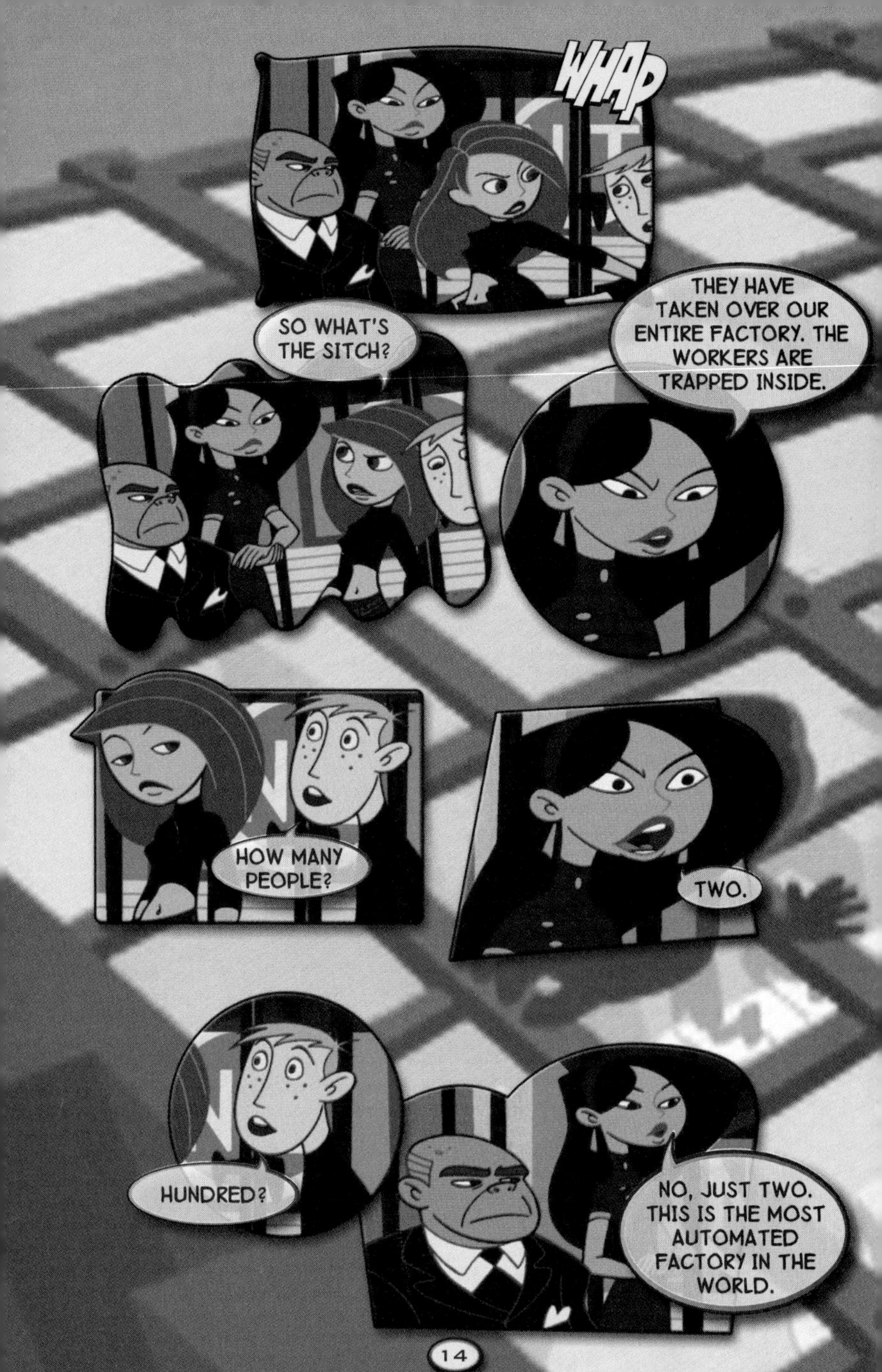
WHAP
SO WHAT'S THE SITCH?
THEY HAVE TAKEN OVER OUR ENTIRE FACTORY. THE WORKERS ARE TRAPPED INSIDE.
HOW MANY PEOPLE?
TWO.
HUNDRED?
NO, JUST TWO. THIS IS THE MOST AUTOMATED FACTORY IN THE WORLD.

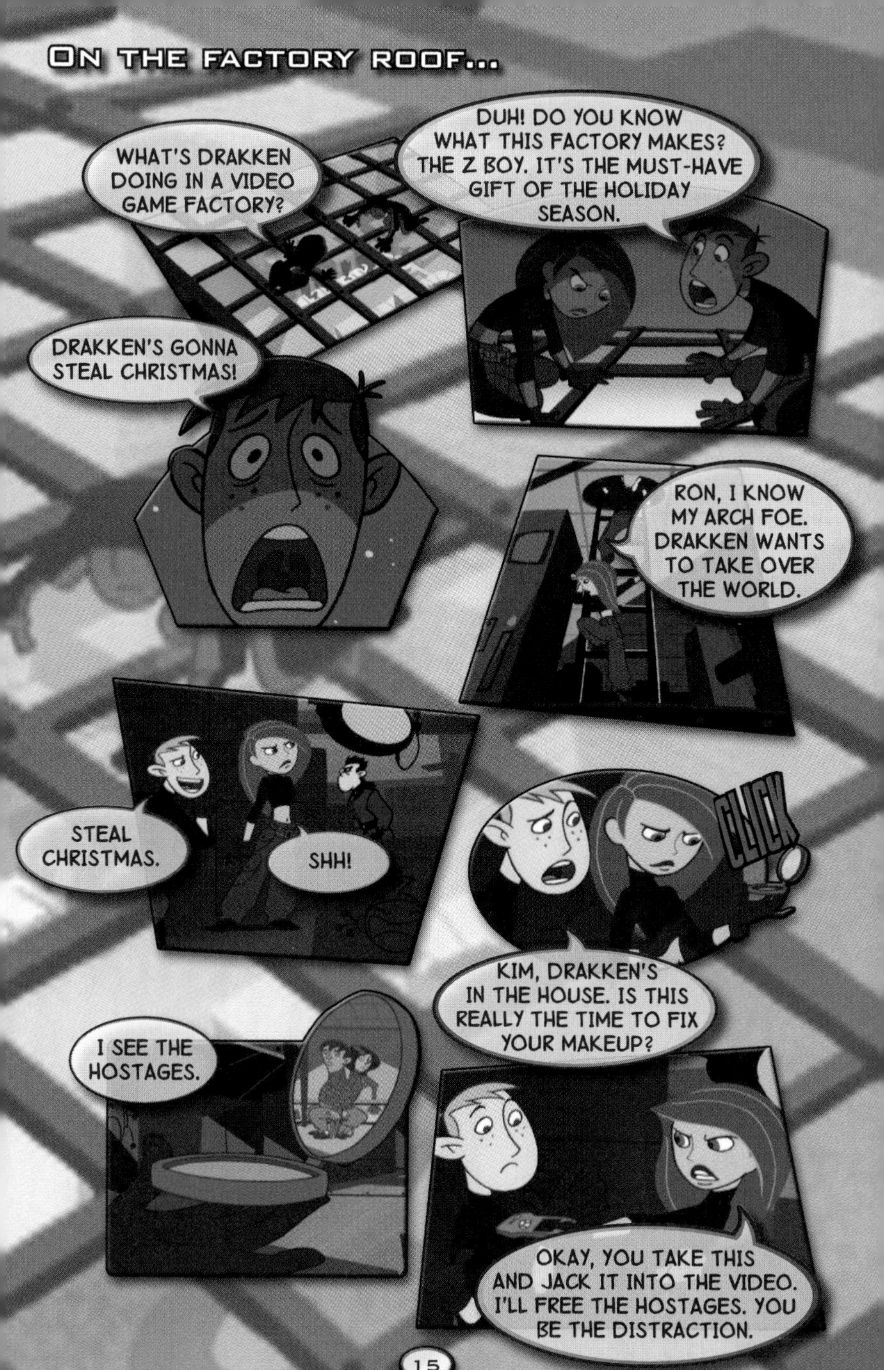
ON THE FACTORY ROOF...
WHAT'S DRAKKEN DOING IN A VIDEO GAME FACTORY?
DUH! DO YOU KNOW WHAT THIS FACTORY MAKES? THE Z BOY. IT'S THE MUST-HAVE GIFT OF THE HOLIDAY SEASON.
DRAKKEN'S GONNA STEAL CHRISTMAS!
RON, I KNOW MY ARCH FOE. DRAKKEN WANTS TO TAKE OVER THE WORLD.
STEAL CHRISTMAS.
SHH!
CLICK
KIM, DRAKKEN'S IN THE HOUSE. IS THIS REALLY THE TIME TO FIX YOUR MAKEUP?
I SEE THE HOSTAGES.
OKAY, YOU TAKE THIS AND JACK IT INTO THE VIDEO. I'LL FREE THE HOSTAGES. YOU BE THE DISTRACTION.

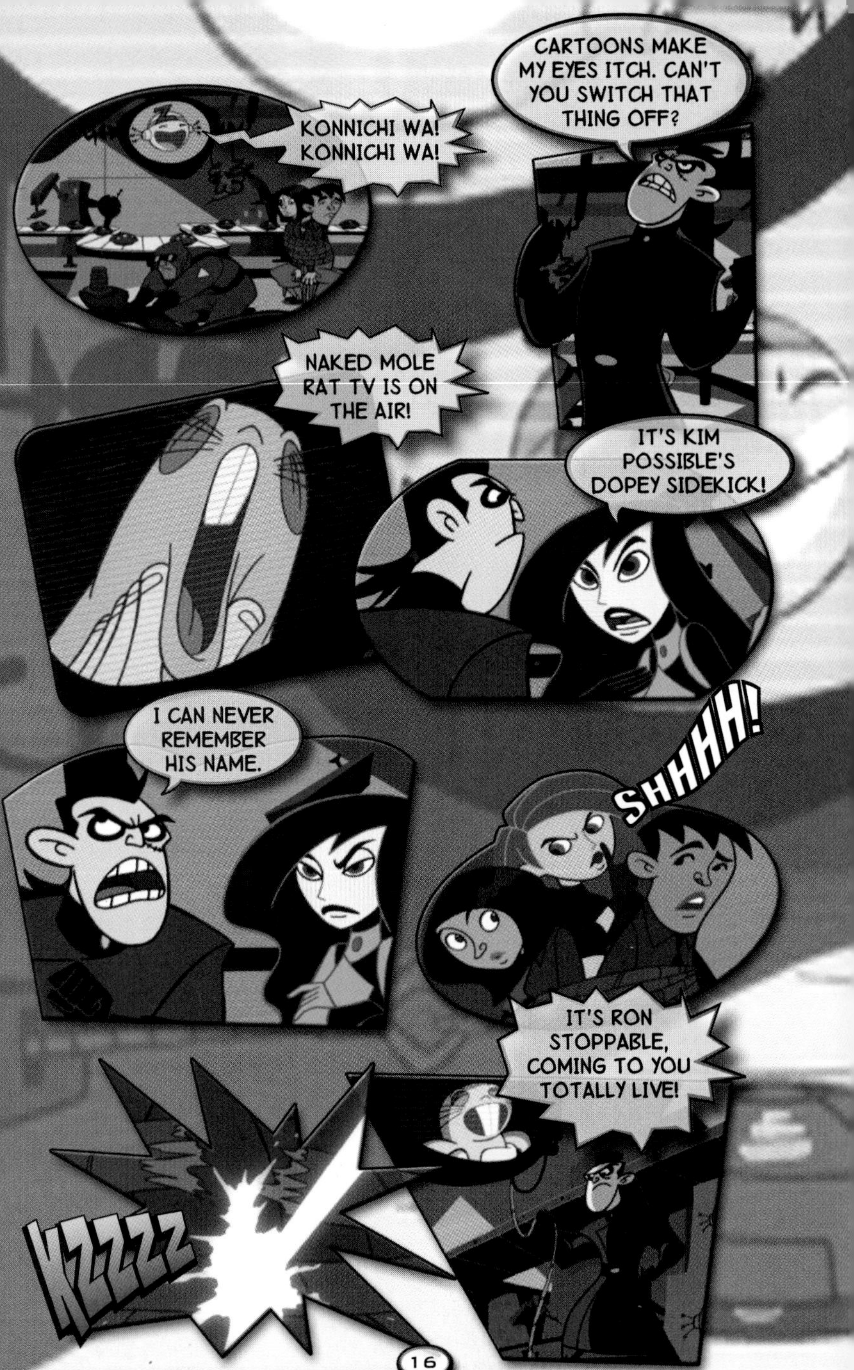
KONNICHI WA! KONNICHI WA!
CARTOONS MAKE MY EYES ITCH. CAN'T YOU SWITCH THAT THING OFF?
NAKED MOLE RAT TV IS ON THE AIR!
IT'S KIM POSSIBLE'S DOPEY SIDEKICK!
I CAN NEVER REMEMBER HIS NAME.
SHHHH!
IT'S RON STOPPABLE, COMING TO YOU TOTALLY LIVE!
KZZZZ

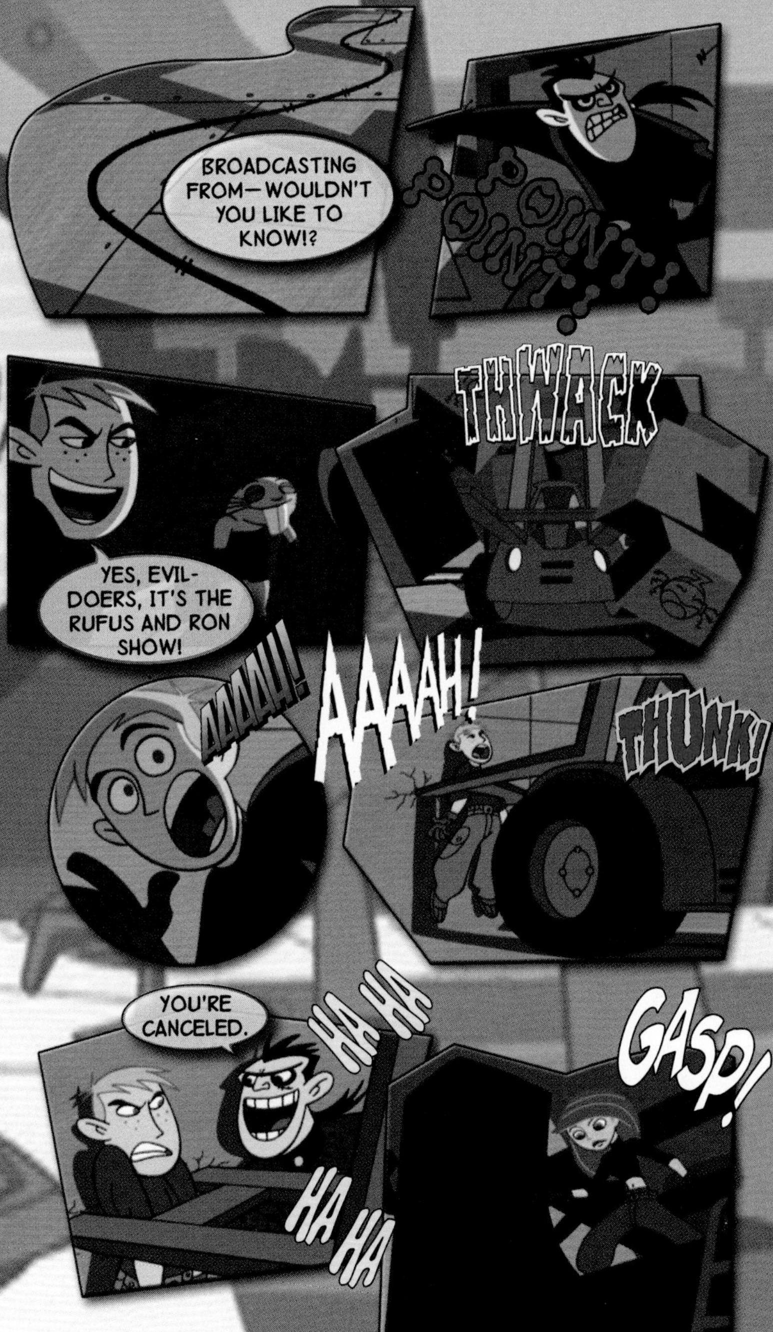
BROADCASTING FROM—WOULDN'T YOU LIKE TO KNOW!?
POINT POINT
YES, EVIL-DOERS, IT'S THE RUFUS AND RON SHOW!
THWACK
AAAAH!
AAAAH!
THUNK!
YOU'RE CANCELED.
HA HA
HA HA
GASP!

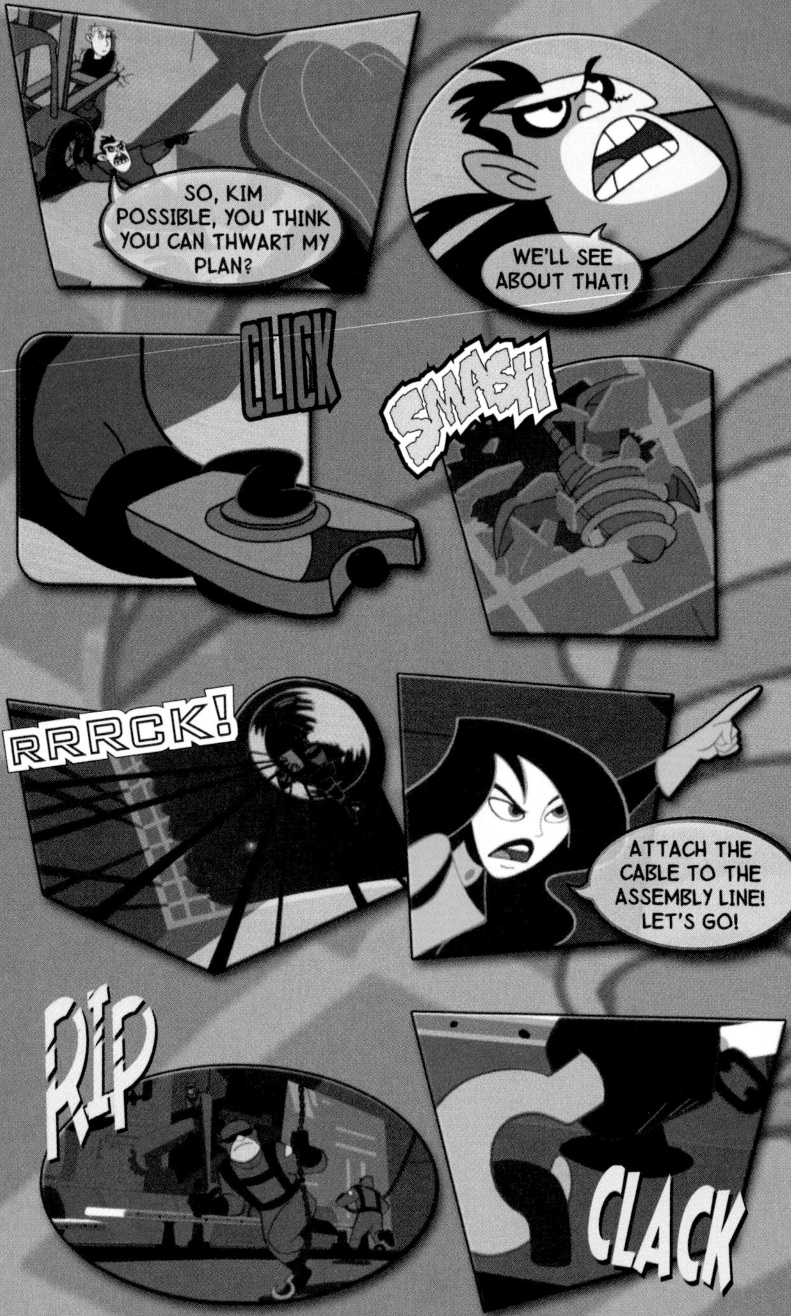
SO, KIM POSSIBLE, YOU THINK YOU CAN THWART MY PLAN?
WE'LL SEE ABOUT THAT!
CLICK
SMASH
RRRCK!
ATTACH THE CABLE TO THE ASSEMBLY LINE! LET'S GO!
RIP
CLACK

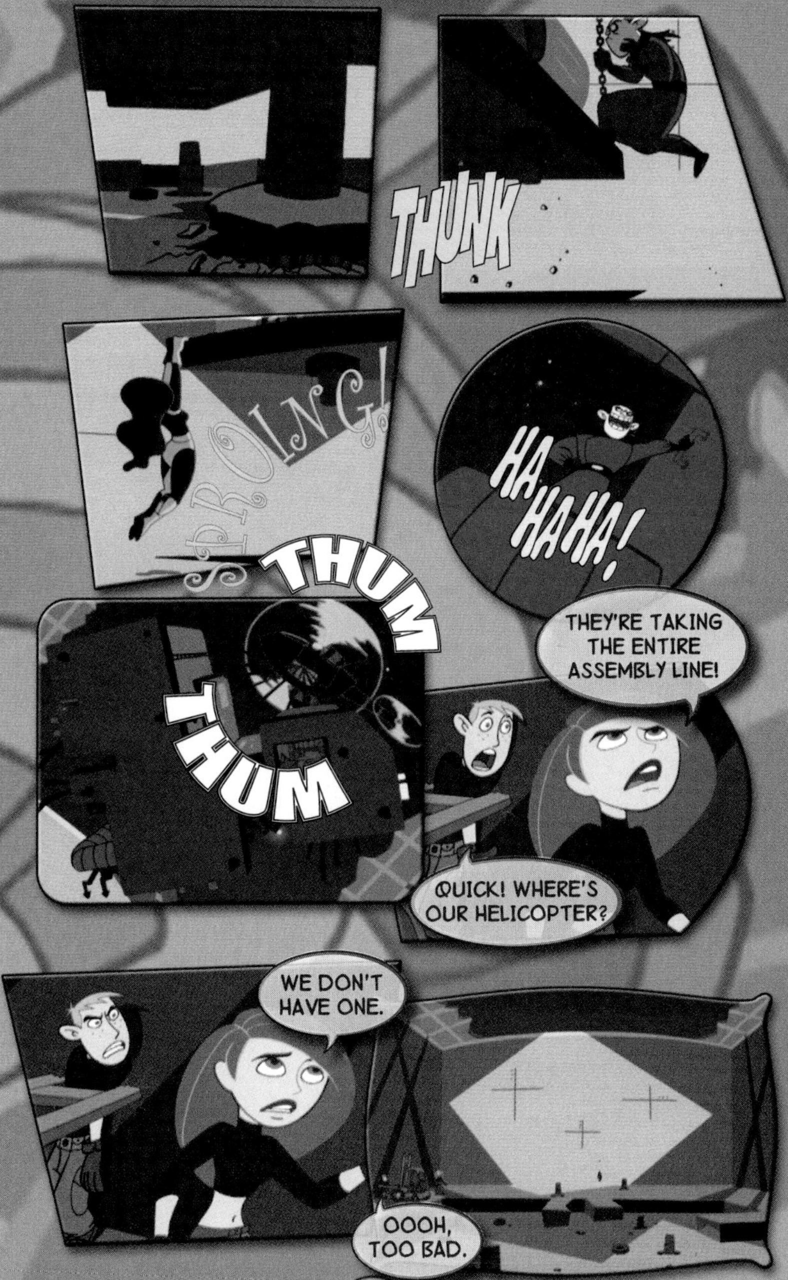
THUNK
SPROING!
HA HAHAHA!
THUM THUM
THEY'RE TAKING THE ENTIRE ASSEMBLY LINE!
QUICK! WHERE'S OUR HELICOPTER?
WE DON'T HAVE ONE.
OOOH, TOO BAD.

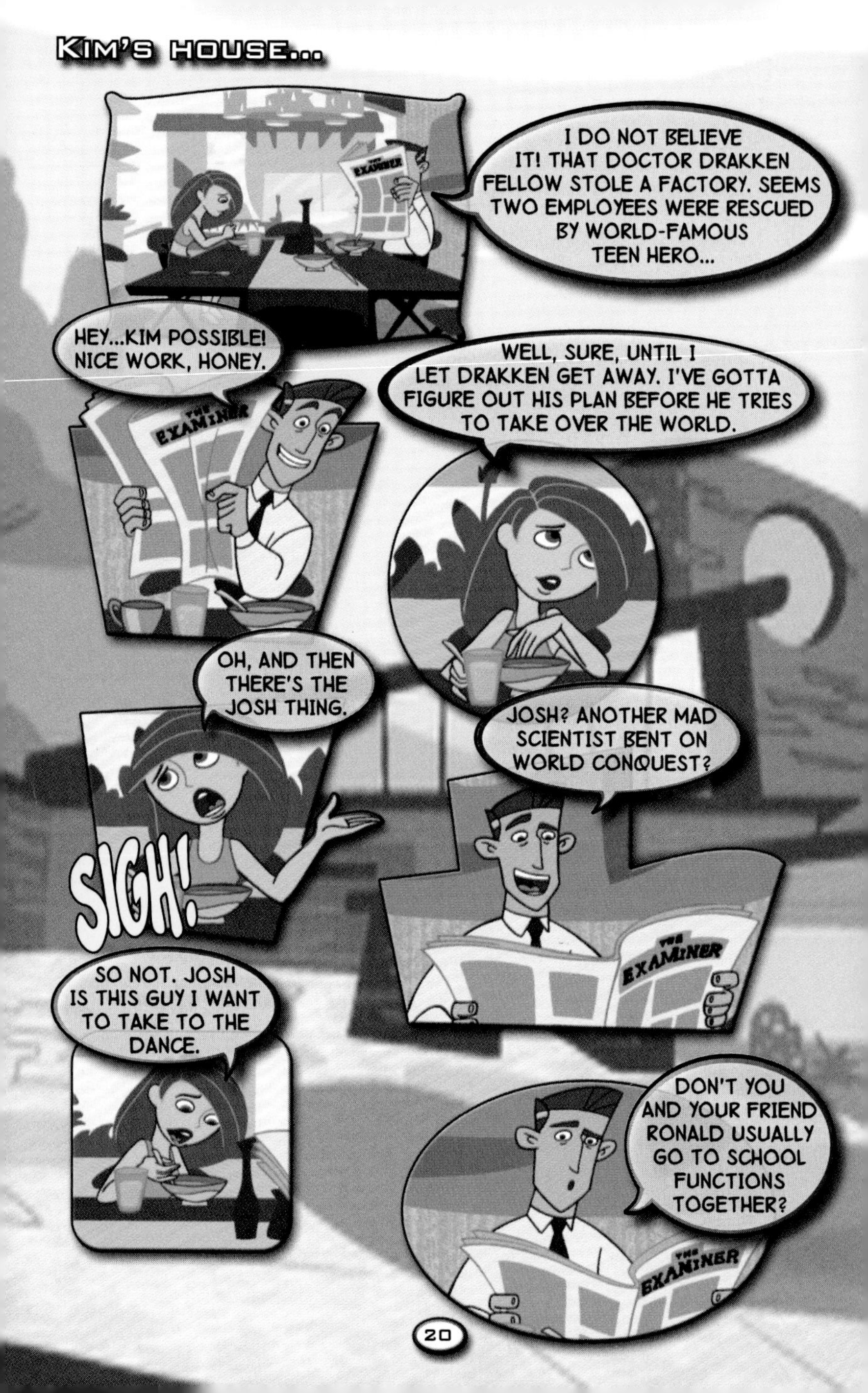
KIM'S HOUSE...
I DO NOT BELIEVE IT! THAT DOCTOR DRAKKEN FELLOW STOLE A FACTORY. SEEMS TWO EMPLOYEES WERE RESCUED BY WORLD-FAMOUS TEEN HERO...
HEY...KIM POSSIBLE! NICE WORK, HONEY.
WELL, SURE, UNTIL I LET DRAKKEN GET AWAY. I'VE GOTTA FIGURE OUT HIS PLAN BEFORE HE TRIES TO TAKE OVER THE WORLD.
OH, AND THEN THERE'S THE JOSH THING.
SIGH!
JOSH? ANOTHER MAD SCIENTIST BENT ON WORLD CONQUEST?
SO NOT. JOSH IS THIS GUY I WANT TO TAKE TO THE DANCE.
DON'T YOU AND YOUR FRIEND RONALD USUALLY GO TO SCHOOL FUNCTIONS TOGETHER?

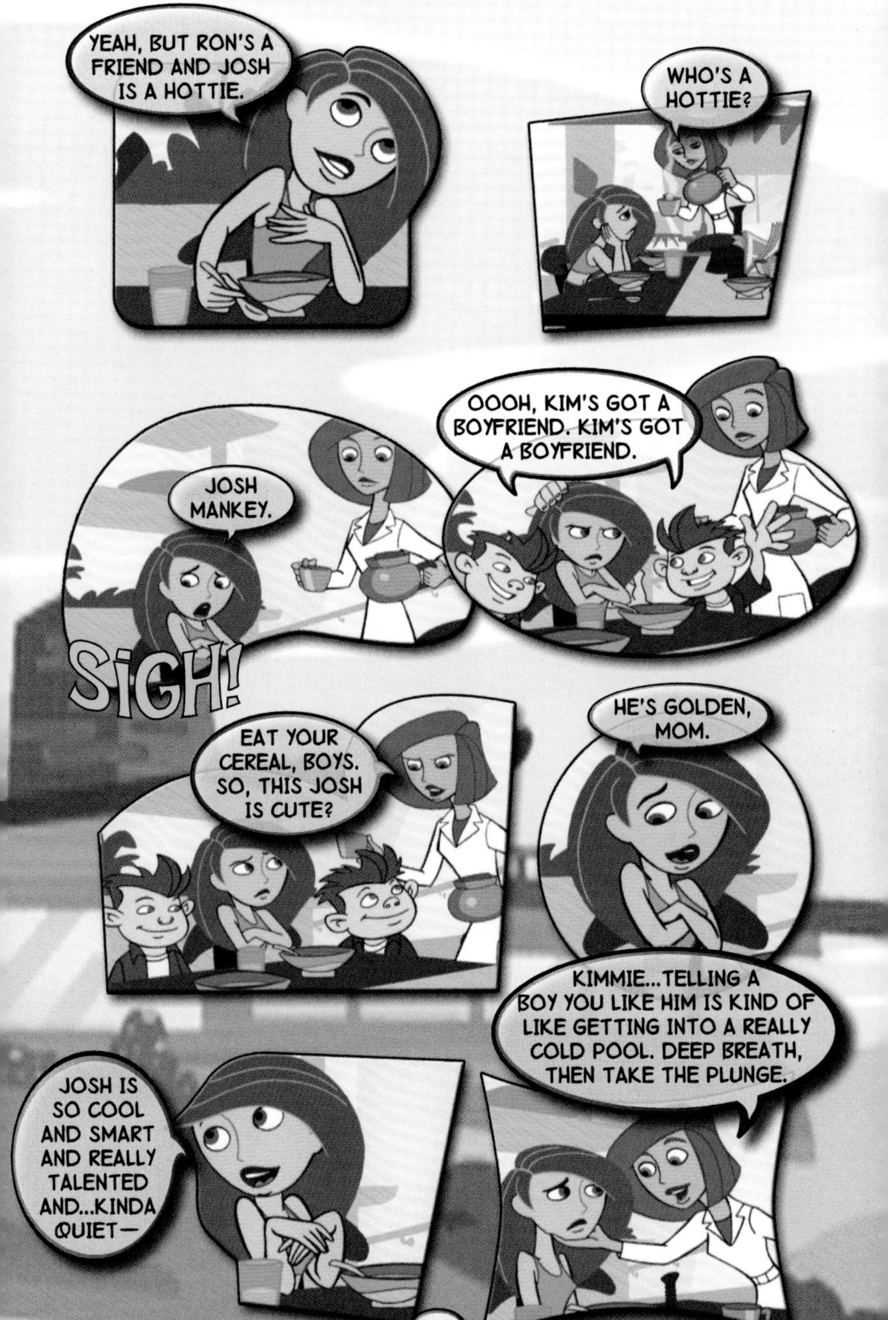

YEAH, BUT RON'S A FRIEND AND JOSH IS A HOTTIE.
WHO'S A HOTTIE?
JOSH MANKEY.
SIGH!
OOOH, KIM'S GOT A BOYFRIEND. KIM'S GOT A BOYFRIEND.
EAT YOUR CEREAL, BOYS. SO, THIS JOSH IS CUTE?
HE'S GOLDEN, MOM.
JOSH IS SO COOL AND SMART AND REALLY TALENTED AND...KINDA QUIET—
KIMMIE...TELLING A BOY YOU LIKE HIM IS KIND OF LIKE GETTING INTO A REALLY COLD POOL. DEEP BREATH, THEN TAKE THE PLUNGE.

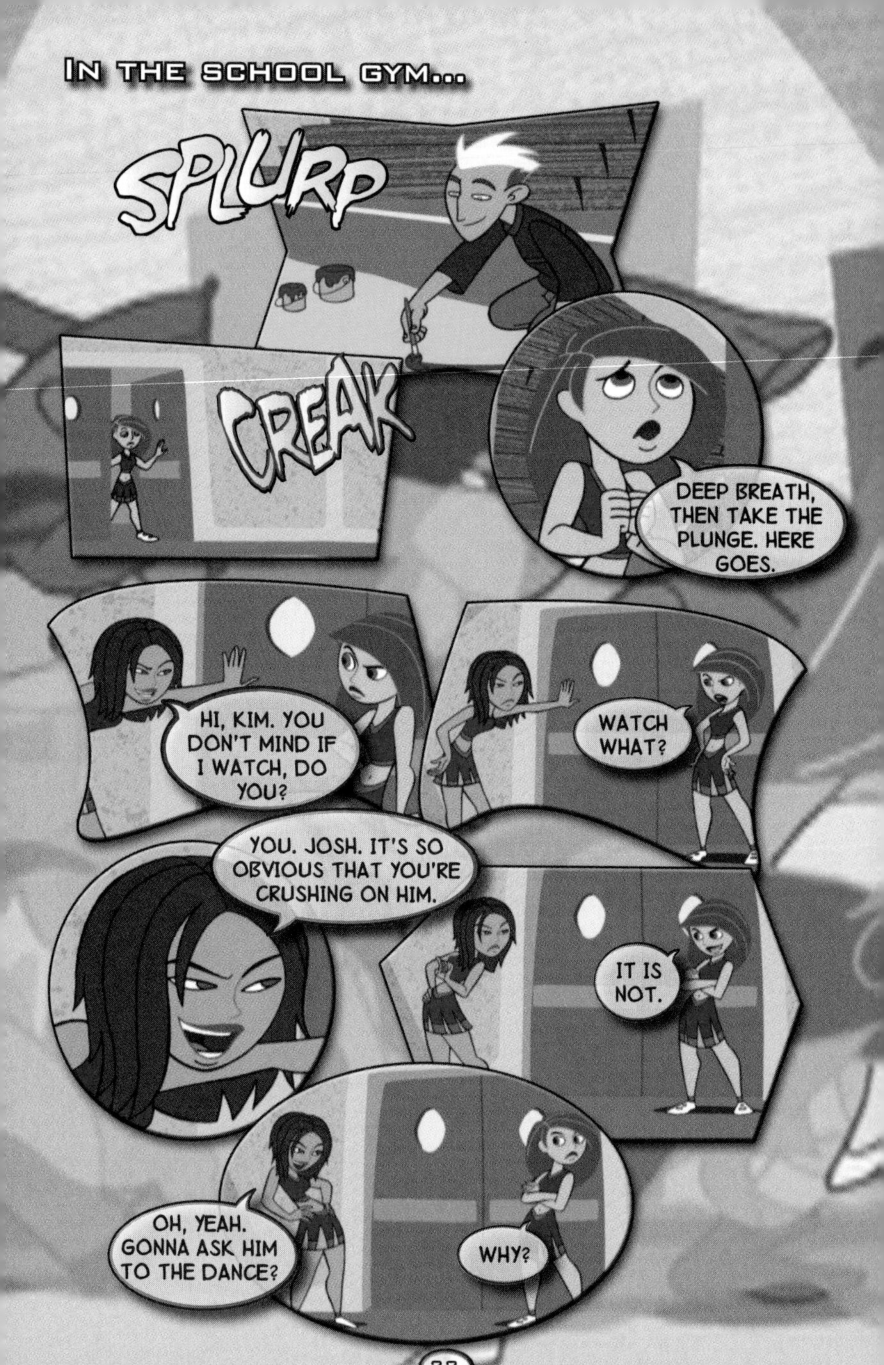
IN THE SCHOOL GYM...
SPLURP
CREAK
DEEP BREATH, THEN TAKE THE PLUNGE. HERE GOES.
HI, KIM. YOU DON'T MIND IF I WATCH, DO YOU?
WATCH WHAT?
YOU. JOSH. IT'S SO OBVIOUS THAT YOU'RE CRUSHING ON HIM.
IT IS NOT.
OH, YEAH. GONNA ASK HIM TO THE DANCE?
WHY?

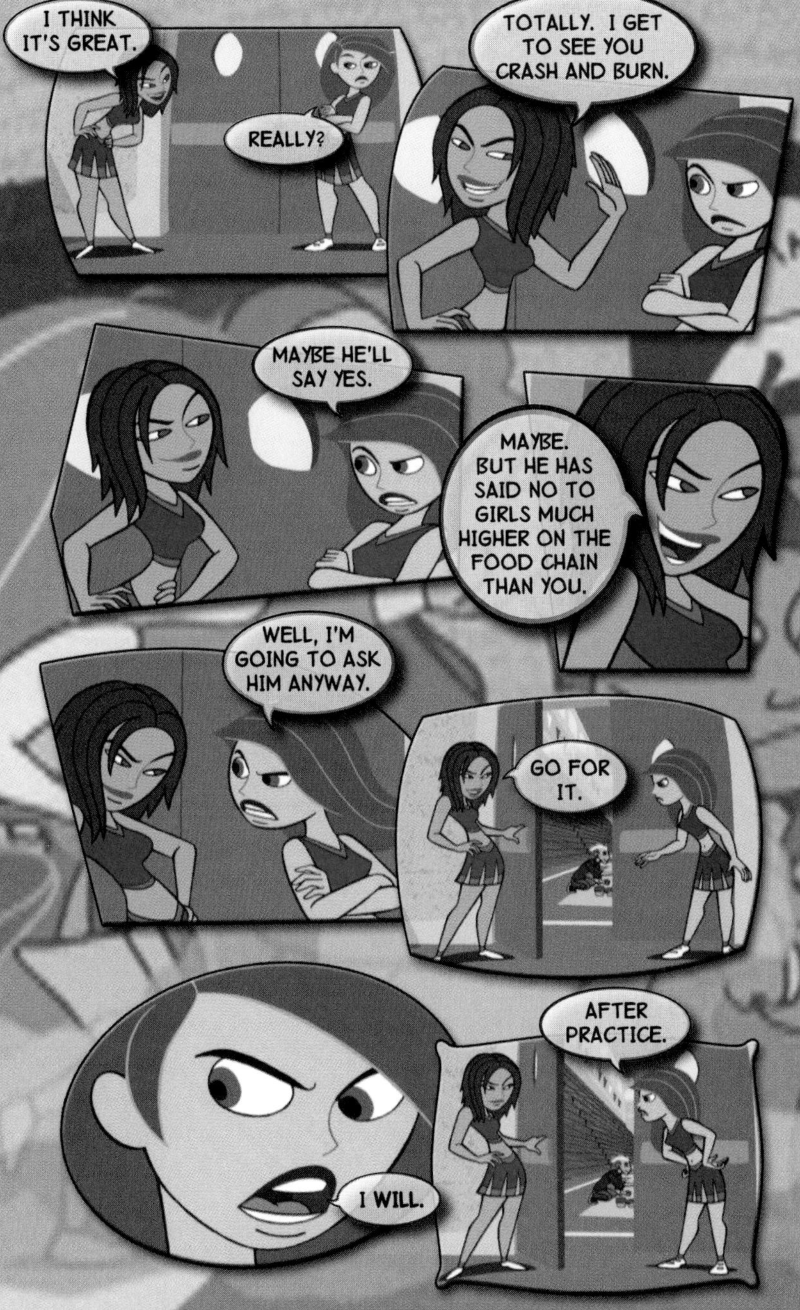
I THINK IT'S GREAT.
REALLY?
TOTALLY. I GET TO SEE YOU CRASH AND BURN.
MAYBE HE'LL SAY YES.
MAYBE. BUT HE HAS SAID NO TO GIRLS MUCH HIGHER ON THE FOOD CHAIN THAN YOU.
WELL, I'M GOING TO ASK HIM ANYWAY.
GO FOR IT.
AFTER PRACTICE.
I WILL.

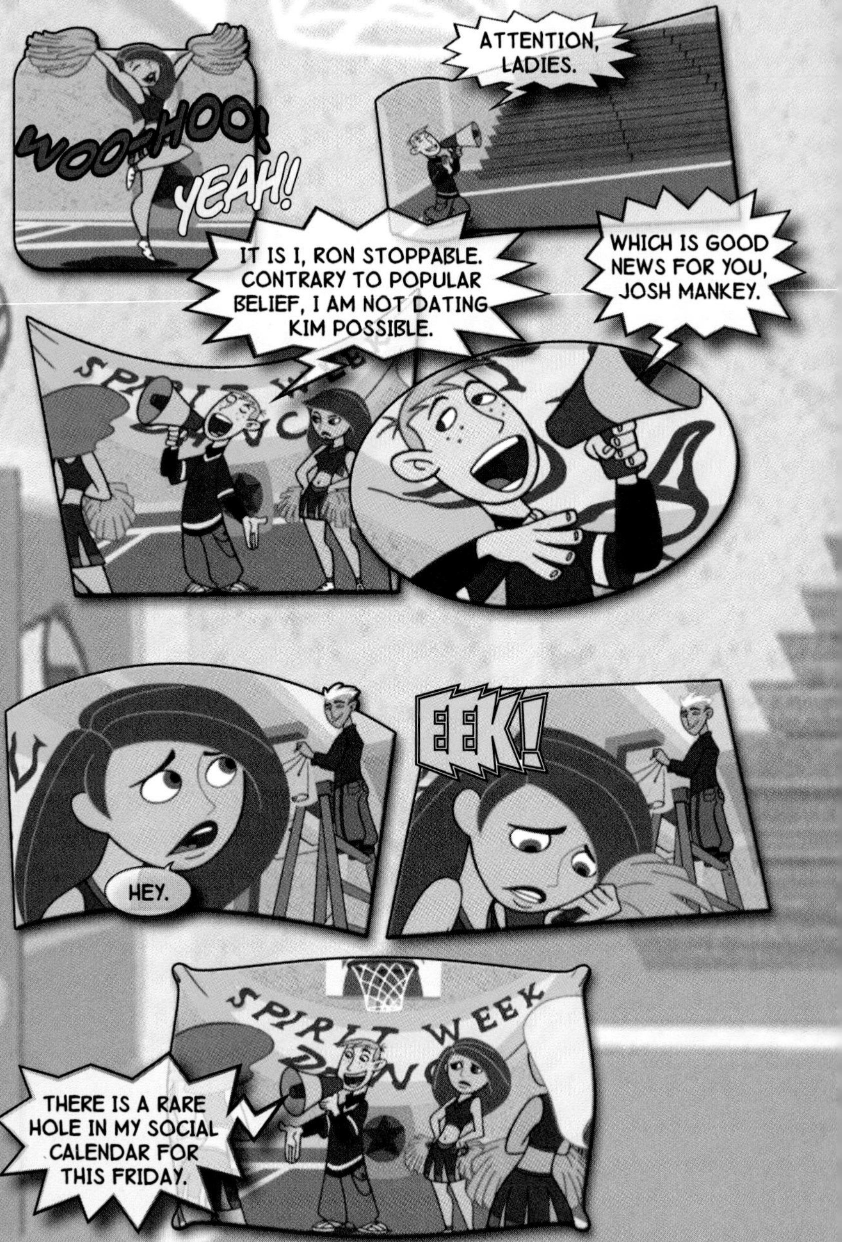
WOO-HOO!
YEAH!
ATTENTION, LADIES.
IT IS I, RON STOPPABLE. CONTRARY TO POPULAR BELIEF, I AM NOT DATING KIM POSSIBLE.
WHICH IS GOOD NEWS FOR YOU, JOSH MANKEY.
SPIRIT WEEK
HEY.
EEK!
SPIRIT WEEK
THERE IS A RARE HOLE IN MY SOCIAL CALENDAR FOR THIS FRIDAY.

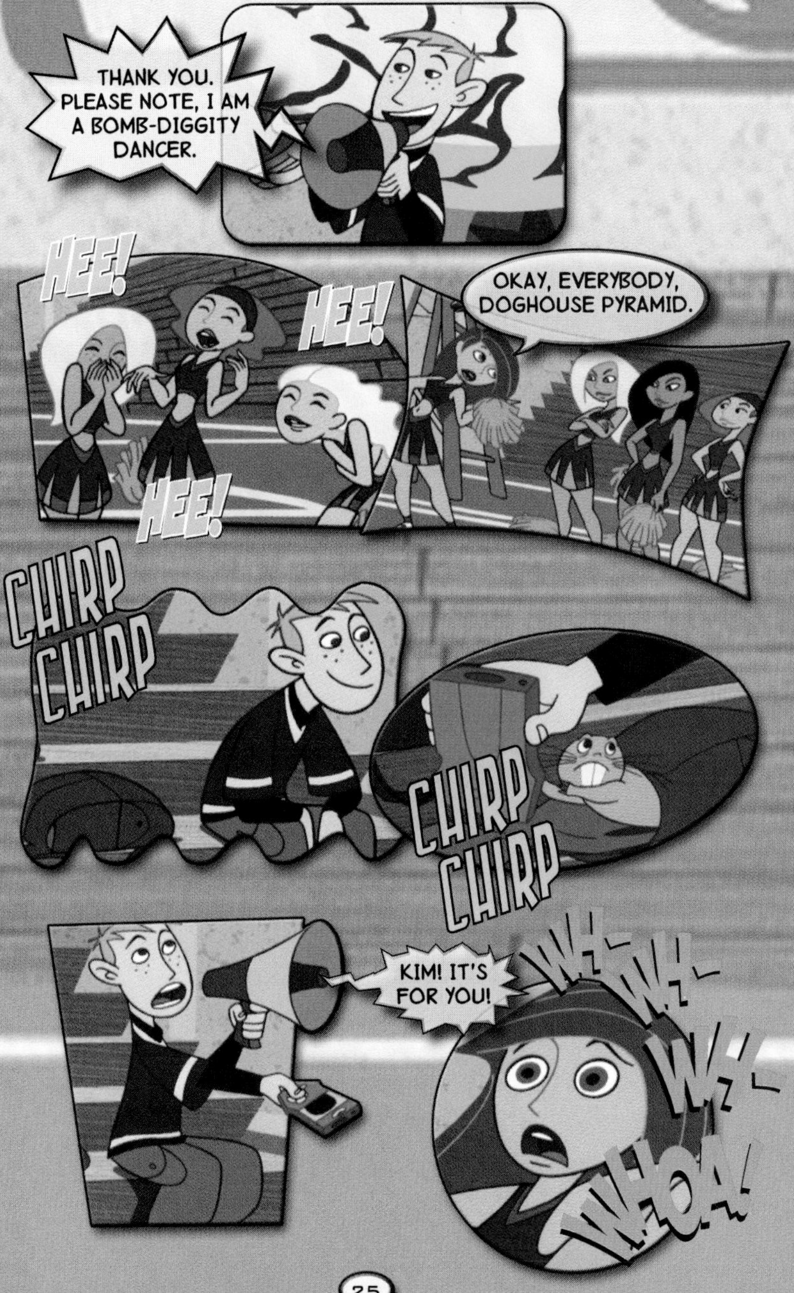

THANK YOU. PLEASE NOTE, I AM A BOMB-DIGGITY DANCER.
HEE!
HEE!
HEE!
OKAY, EVERYBODY, DOGHOUSE PYRAMID.
CHIRP CHIRP
CHIRP CHIRP
KIM! IT'S FOR YOU!
WH-WH-WH-WHOA!

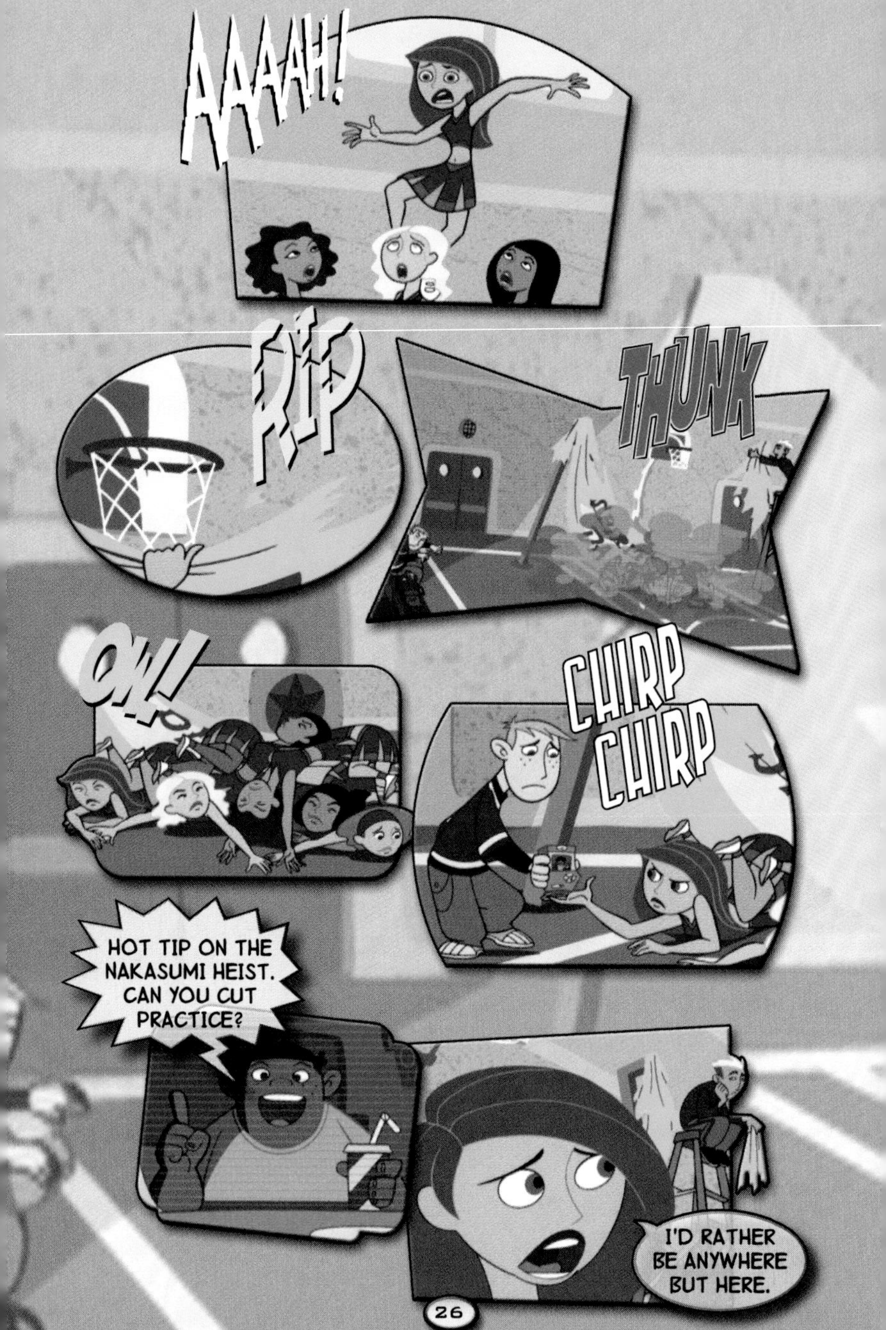
AAAAH!
RIP
THUNK
OW!
CHIRP
CHIRP
HOT TIP ON THE NAKASUMI HEIST. CAN YOU CUT PRACTICE?
I'D RATHER BE ANYWHERE BUT HERE.

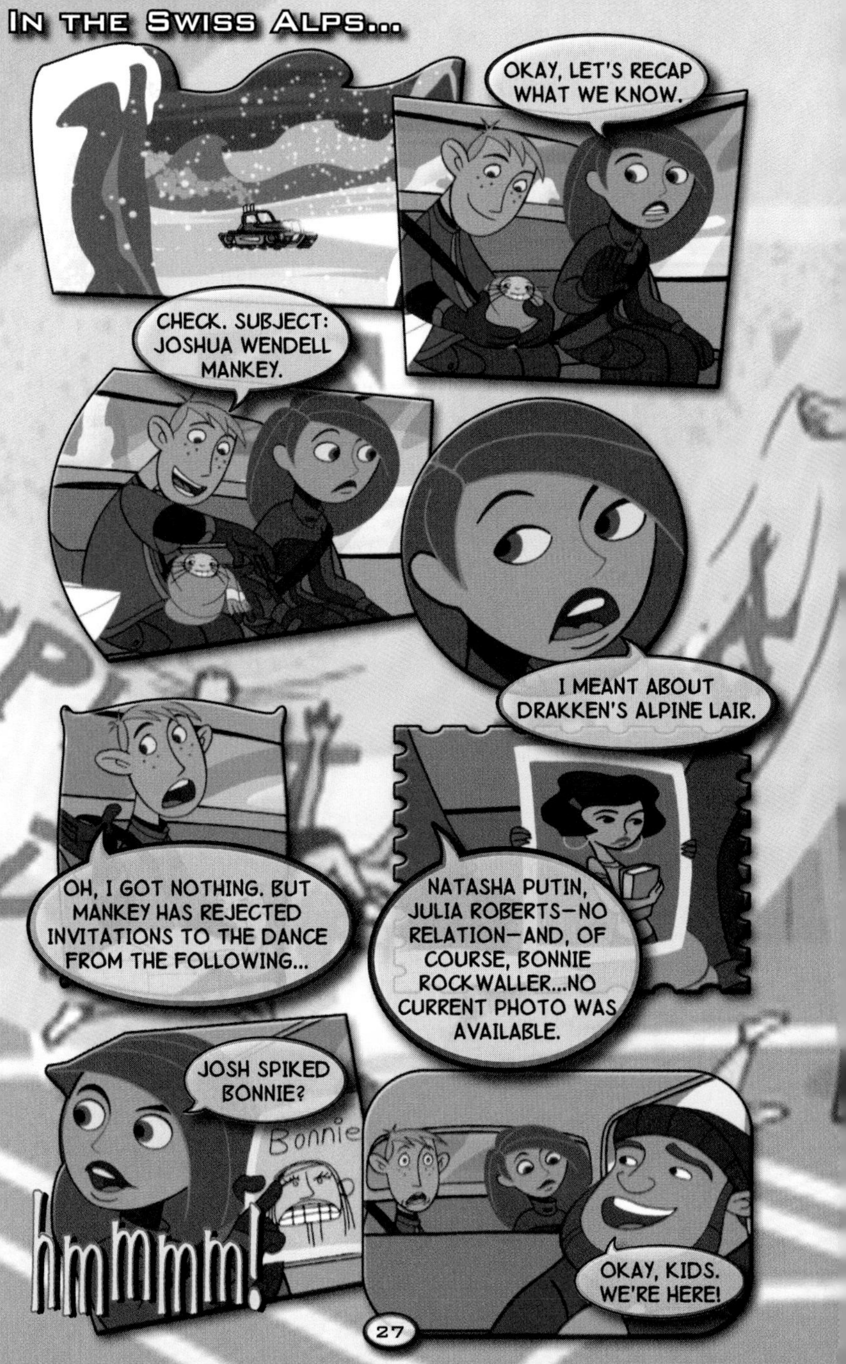
IN THE SWISS ALPS...
OKAY, LET'S RECAP WHAT WE KNOW.
CHECK. SUBJECT: JOSHUA WENDELL MANKEY.
I MEANT ABOUT DRAKKEN'S ALPINE LAIR.
OH, I GOT NOTHING. BUT MANKEY HAS REJECTED INVITATIONS TO THE DANCE FROM THE FOLLOWING...
NATASHA PUTIN, JULIA ROBERTS—NO RELATION—AND, OF COURSE, BONNIE ROCKWALLER...NO CURRENT PHOTO WAS AVAILABLE.
JOSH SPIKED BONNIE?
Bonnie
hmmmm!
OKAY, KIDS. WE'RE HERE!

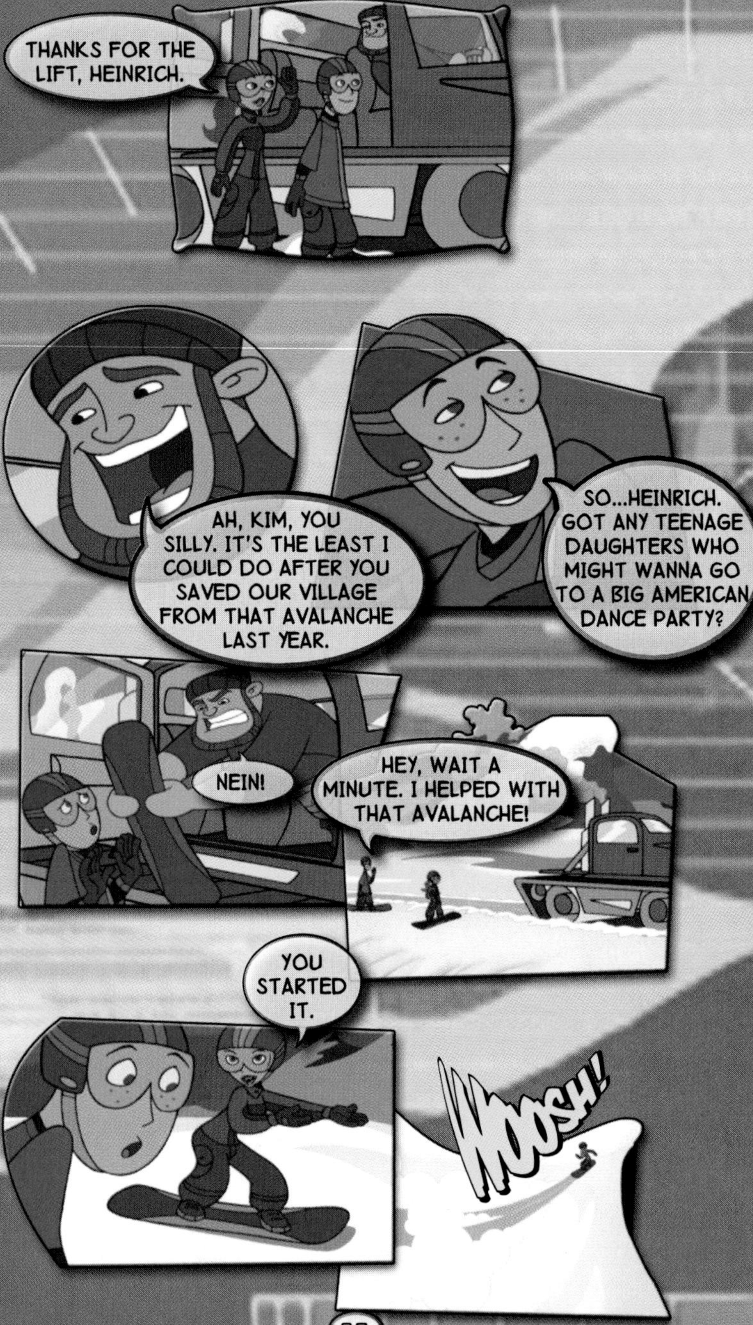
THANKS FOR THE LIFT, HEINRICH.
AH, KIM, YOU SILLY. IT'S THE LEAST I COULD DO AFTER YOU SAVED OUR VILLAGE FROM THAT AVALANCHE LAST YEAR.
SO...HEINRICH. GOT ANY TEENAGE DAUGHTERS WHO MIGHT WANNA GO TO A BIG AMERICAN DANCE PARTY?
NEIN!
HEY, WAIT A MINUTE. I HELPED WITH THAT AVALANCHE!
YOU STARTED IT.
WOOSH!

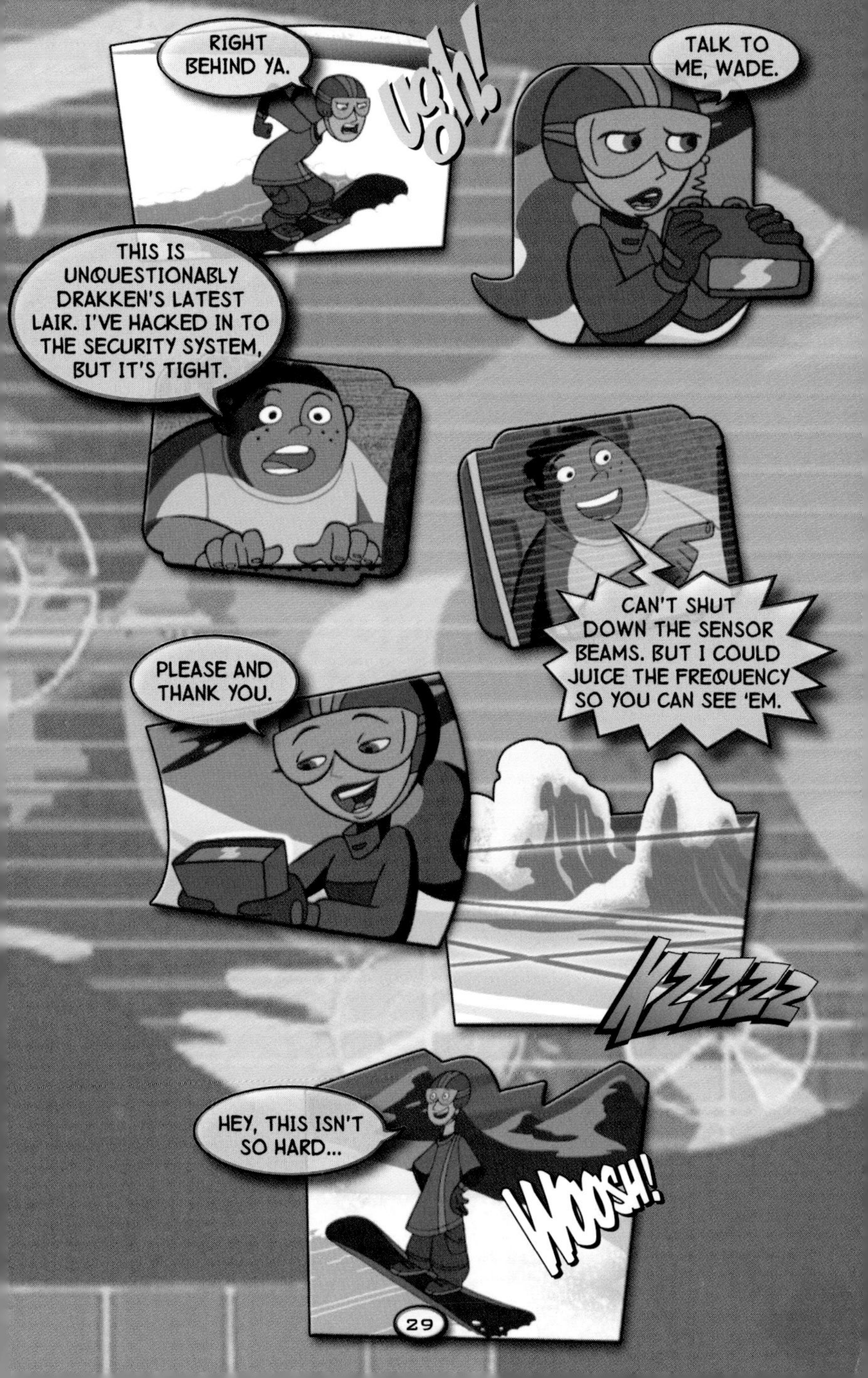

RIGHT BEHIND YA.
UGH!
TALK TO ME, WADE.
THIS IS UNQUESTIONABLY DRAKKEN'S LATEST LAIR. I'VE HACKED IN TO THE SECURITY SYSTEM, BUT IT'S TIGHT.
CAN'T SHUT DOWN THE SENSOR BEAMS. BUT I COULD JUICE THE FREQUENCY SO YOU CAN SEE 'EM.
PLEASE AND THANK YOU.
KZZZZ
HEY, THIS ISN'T SO HARD...
WOOSH!

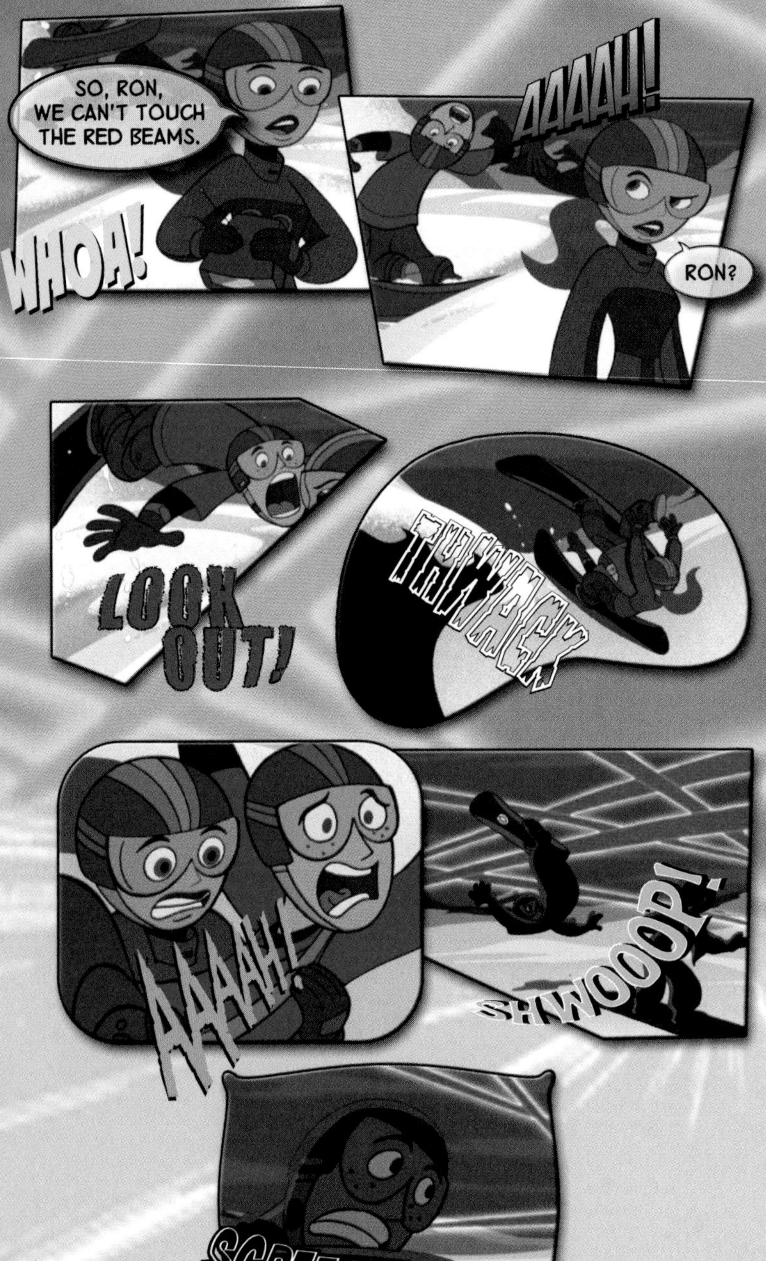
SO, RON, WE CAN'T TOUCH THE RED BEAMS.
WHOA!
AAAAH!
RON?
LOOK OUT!
THWACK
AAAAH!
SHWOOOP!
SCREECH

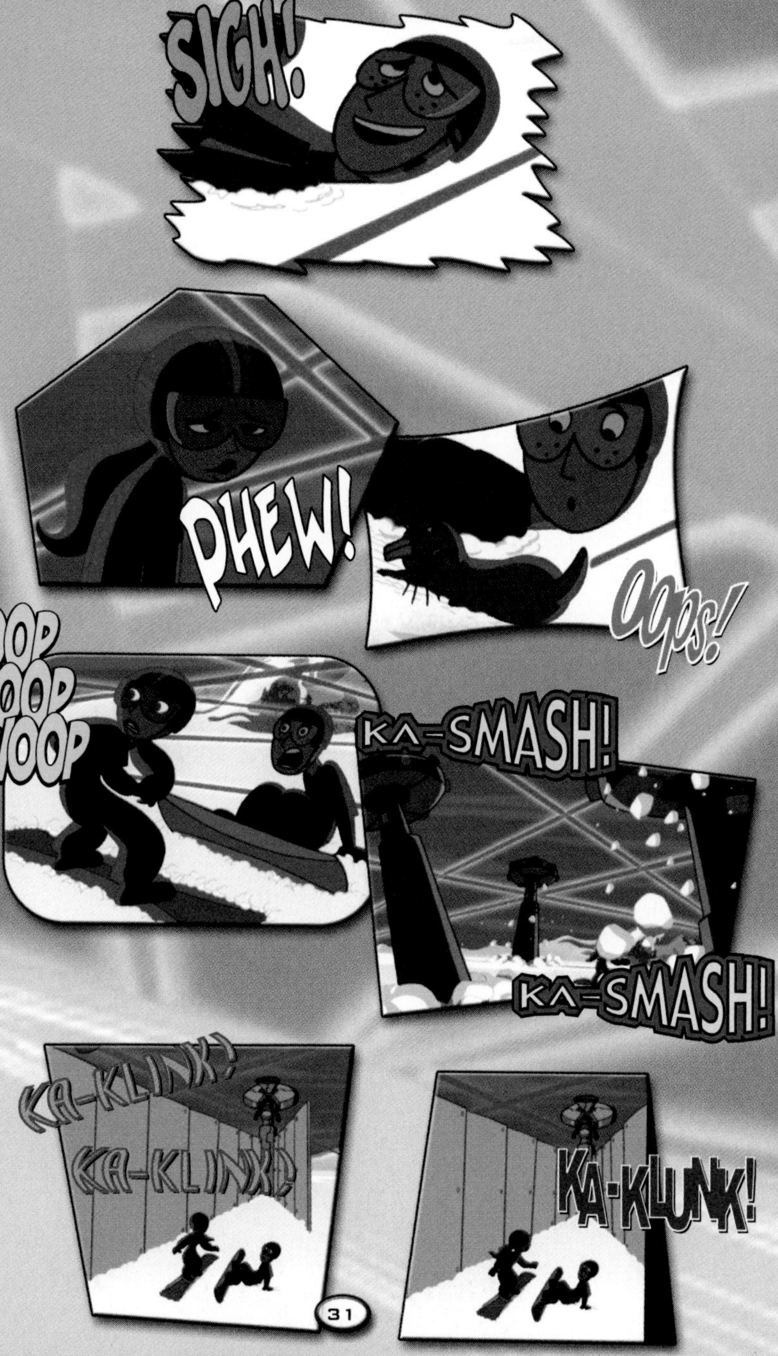
SIGH!
PHEW!
Oops!
WOOP
WOOP
WOOP
KA-SMASH!
KA-SMASH!
KA-KLINK!
KA-KLINK!
KA-KLUNK!

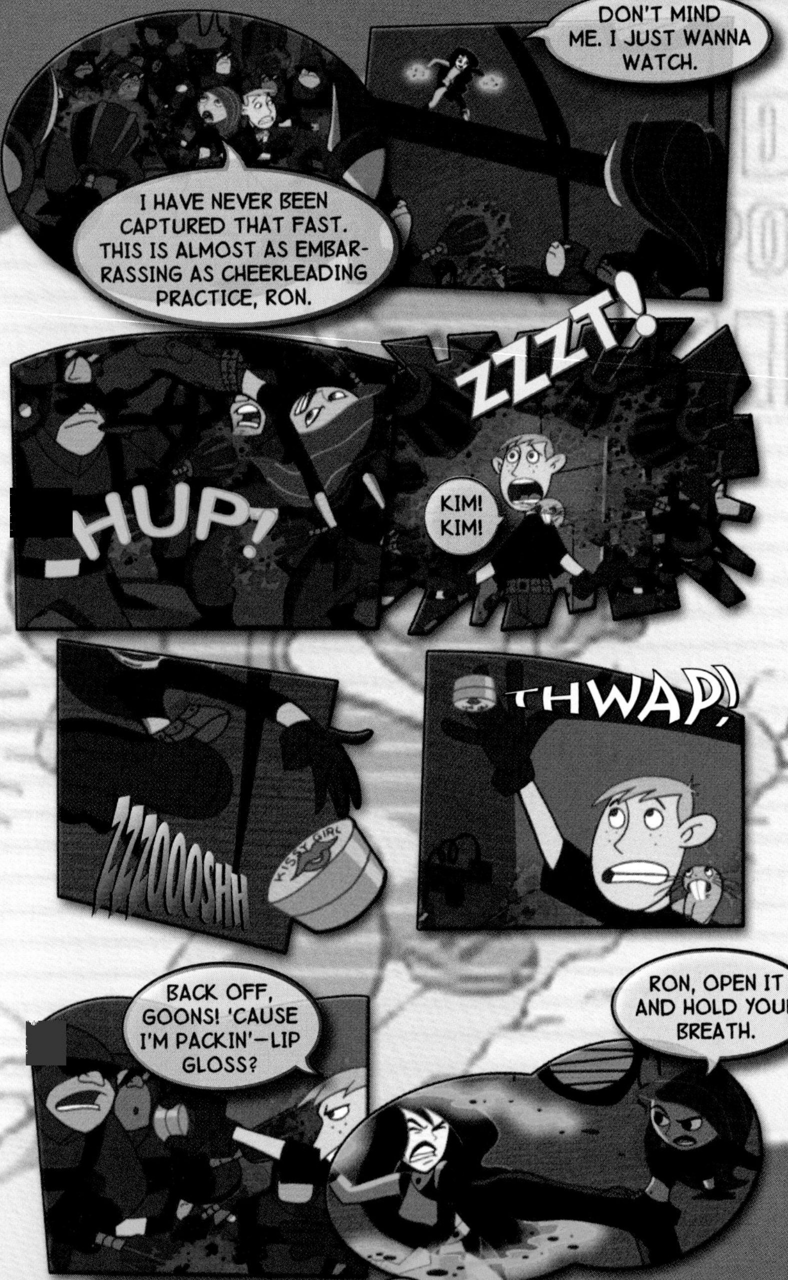
I HAVE NEVER BEEN CAPTURED THAT FAST. THIS IS ALMOST AS EMBARRASSING AS CHEERLEADING PRACTICE, RON.
DON'T MIND ME. I JUST WANNA WATCH.
HUP!
ZZZZT!
KIM! KIM!
ZZZOOOSHH
THWAP!
BACK OFF, GOONS! 'CAUSE I'M PACKIN'—LIP GLOSS?
RON, OPEN IT AND HOLD YOUR BREATH.

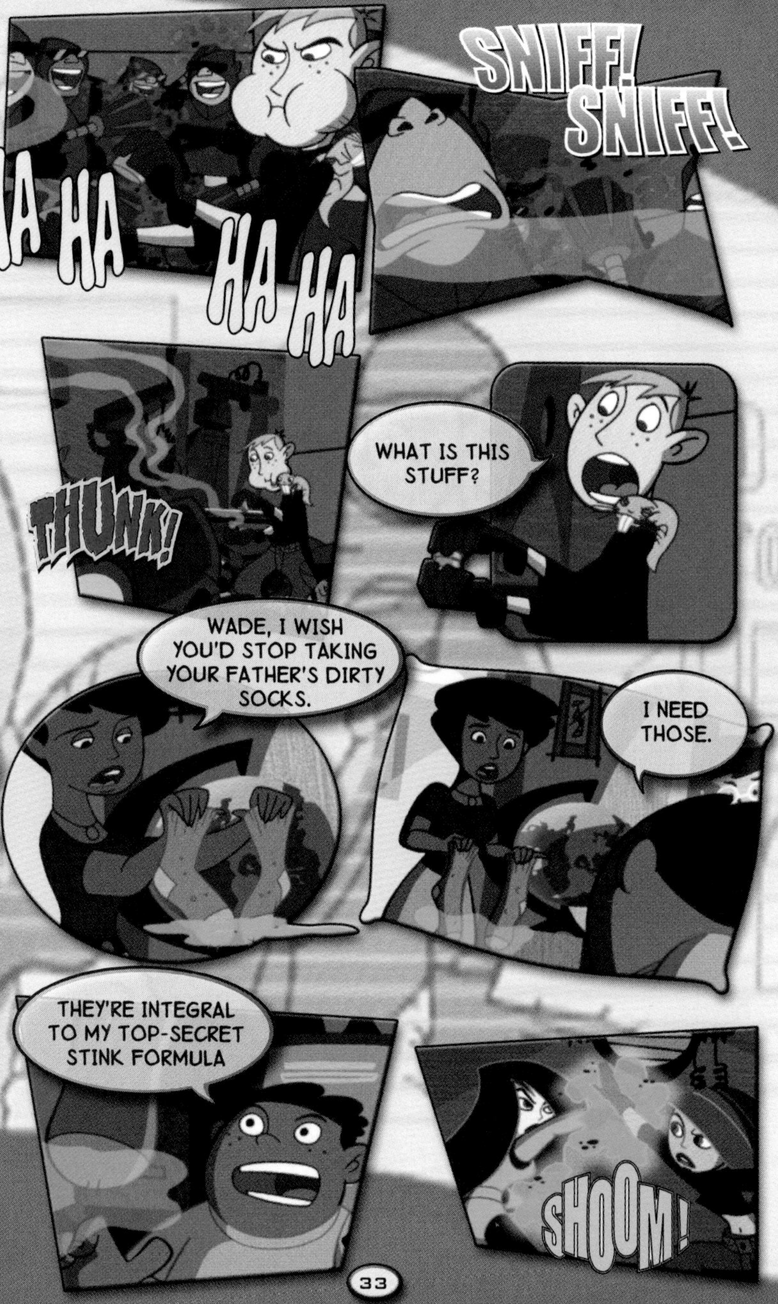
HA HA
HA HA
SNIFF! SNIFF!
THUNK!
WHAT IS THIS STUFF?
WADE, I WISH YOU'D STOP TAKING YOUR FATHER'S DIRTY SOCKS.
I NEED THOSE.
THEY'RE INTEGRAL TO MY TOP-SECRET STINK FORMULA
SHOOM!

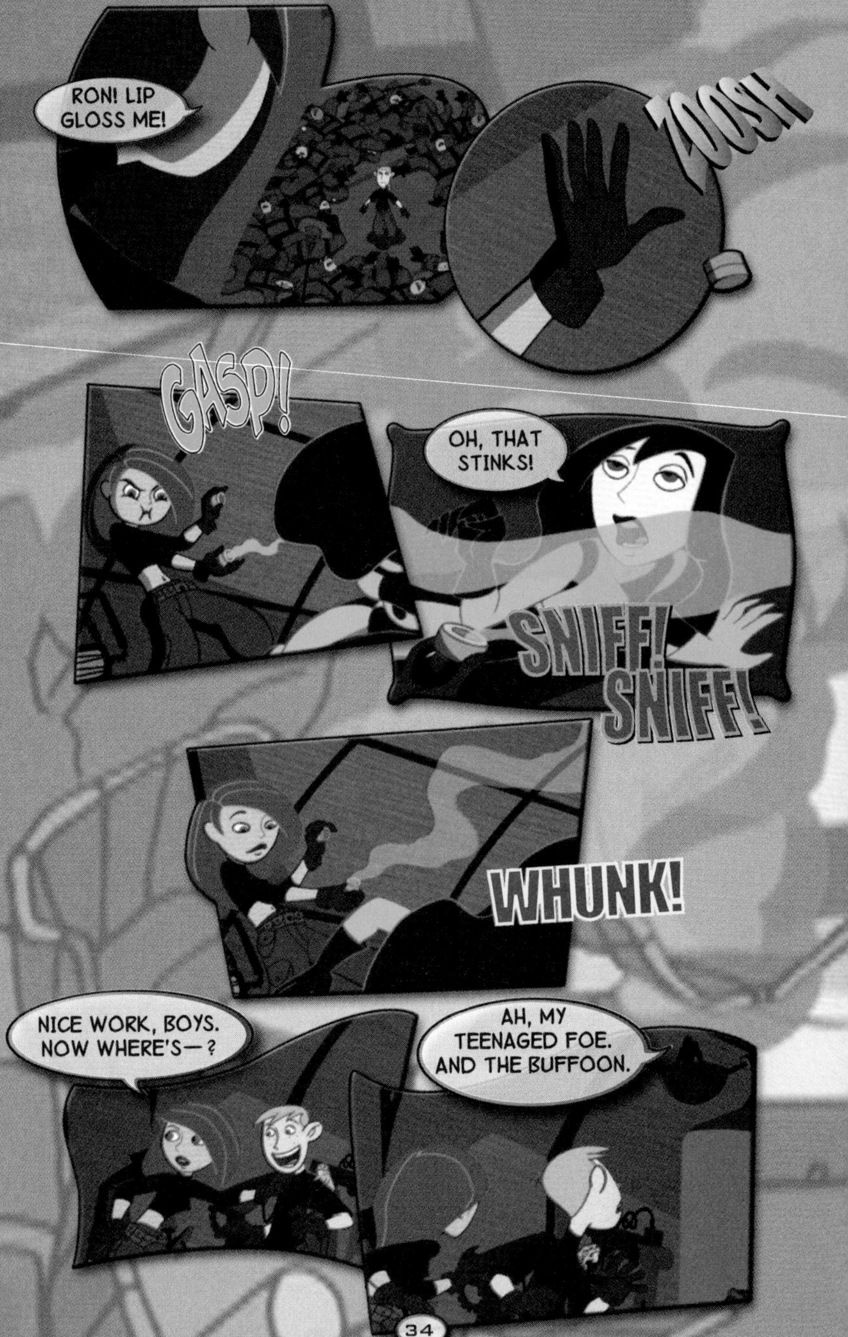
RON! LIP GLOSS ME!
ZOOSH
GASP!
OH, THAT STINKS!
SNIFF! SNIFF!
WHUNK!
NICE WORK, BOYS. NOW WHERE'S— ?
AH, MY TEENAGED FOE. AND THE BUFFOON.

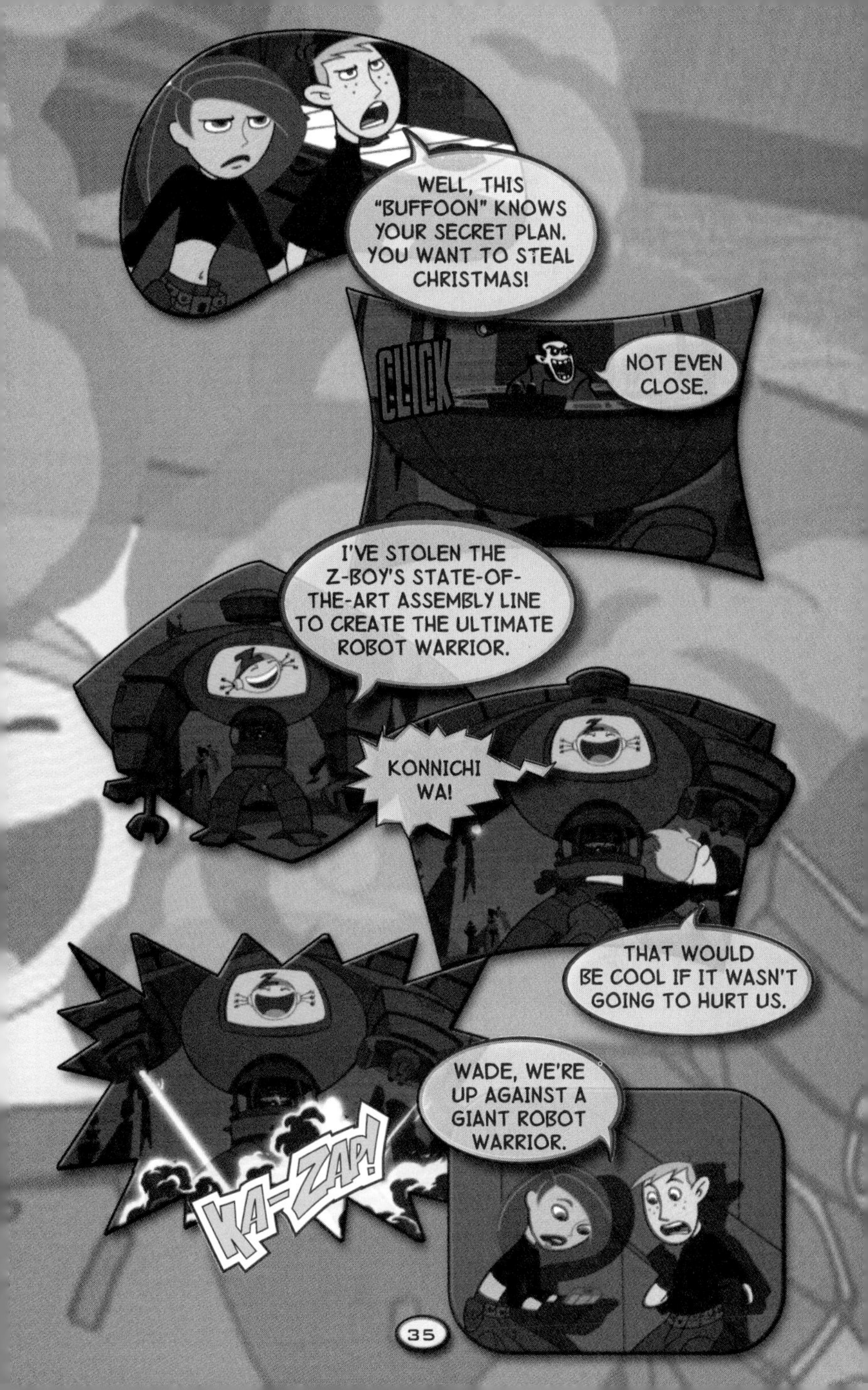
WELL, THIS "BUFFOON" KNOWS YOUR SECRET PLAN. YOU WANT TO STEAL CHRISTMAS!
CLICK
NOT EVEN CLOSE.
I'VE STOLEN THE Z-BOY'S STATE-OF-THE-ART ASSEMBLY LINE TO CREATE THE ULTIMATE ROBOT WARRIOR.
KONNICHI WA!
THAT WOULD BE COOL IF IT WASN'T GOING TO HURT US.
WADE, WE'RE UP AGAINST A GIANT ROBOT WARRIOR.
KA-ZAP!

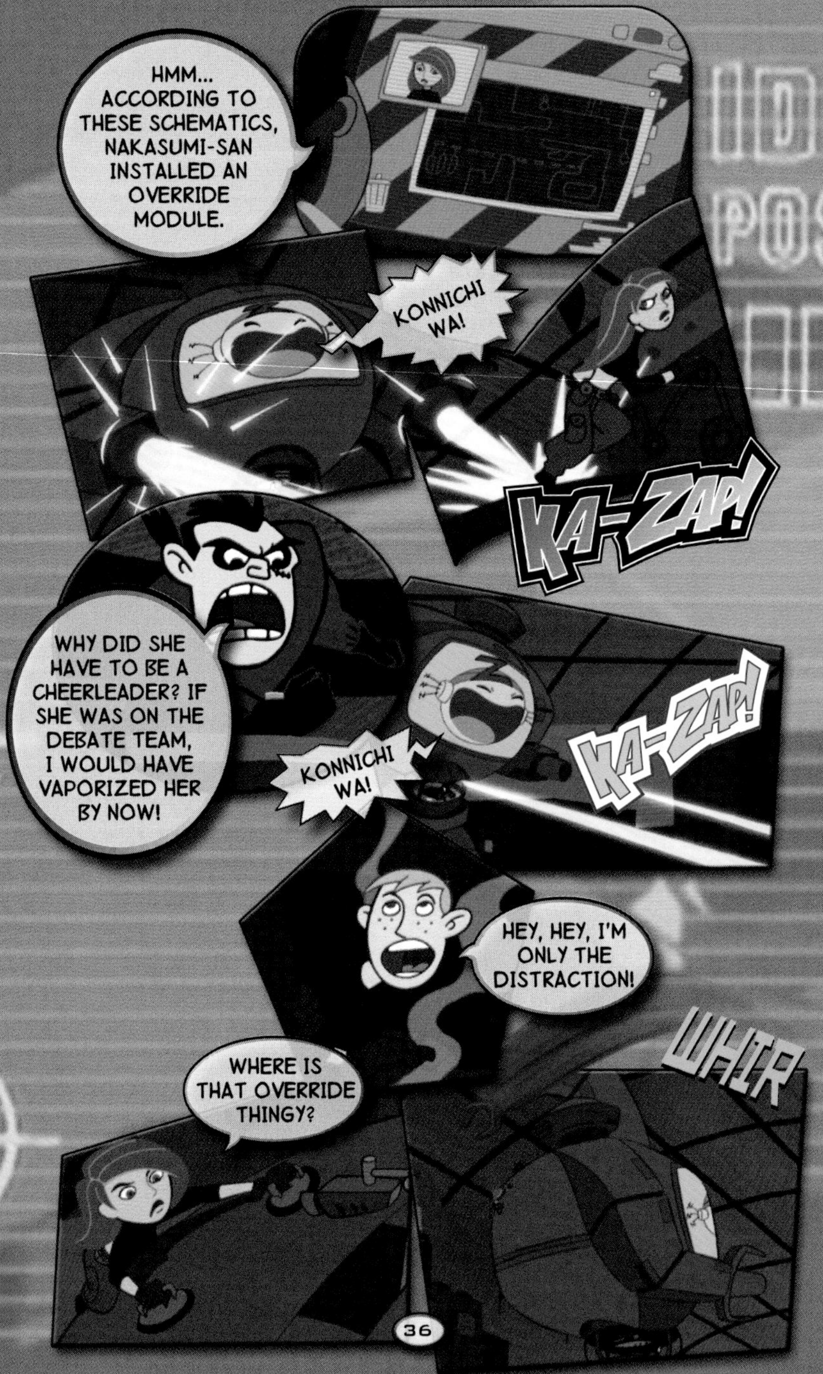
HMM... ACCORDING TO THESE SCHEMATICS, NAKASUMI-SAN INSTALLED AN OVERRIDE MODULE.
KONNICHI WA!
KA-ZAP!
WHY DID SHE HAVE TO BE A CHEERLEADER? IF SHE WAS ON THE DEBATE TEAM, I WOULD HAVE VAPORIZED HER BY NOW!
KONNICHI WA!
KA-ZAP!
HEY, HEY, I'M ONLY THE DISTRACTION!
WHIR
WHERE IS THAT OVERRIDE THINGY?

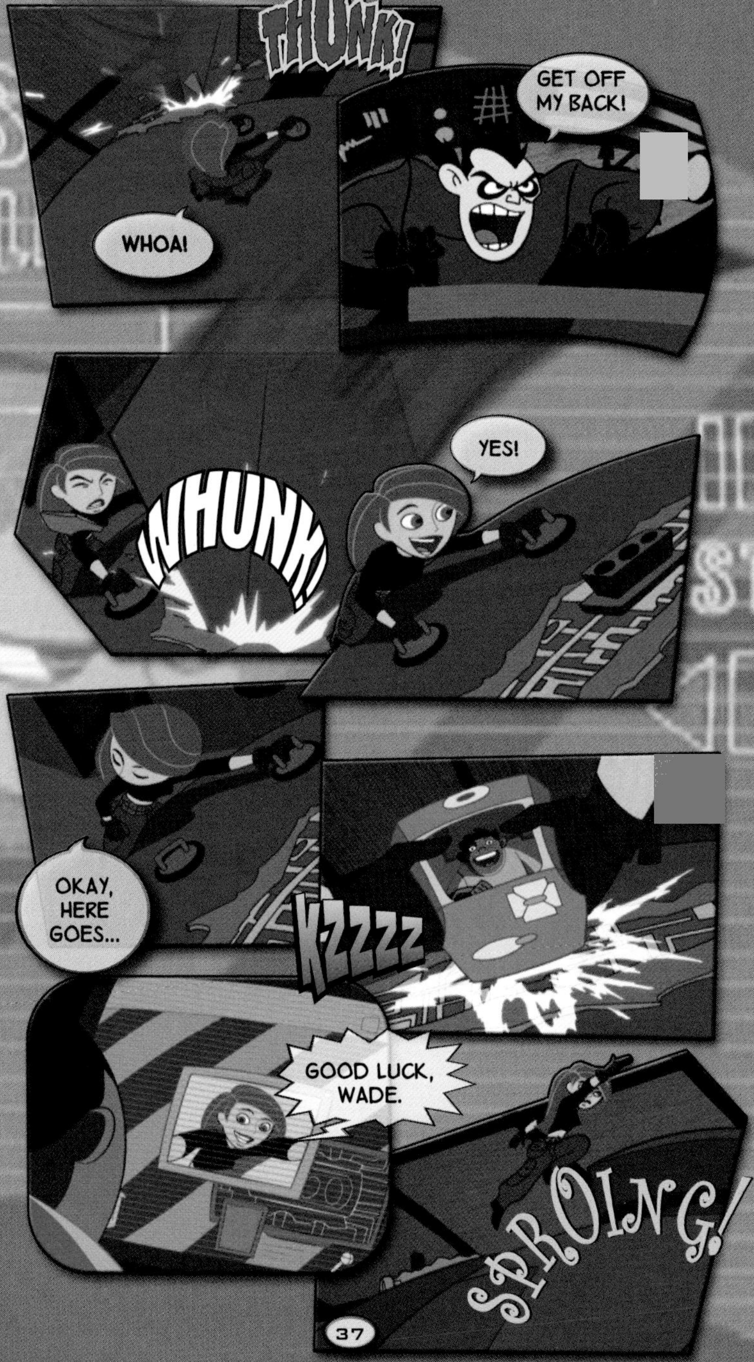
THUNK!
WHOA!
GET OFF MY BACK!
WHUNK!
YES!
OKAY, HERE GOES...
KZZZZ
GOOD LUCK, WADE.
SPROING!

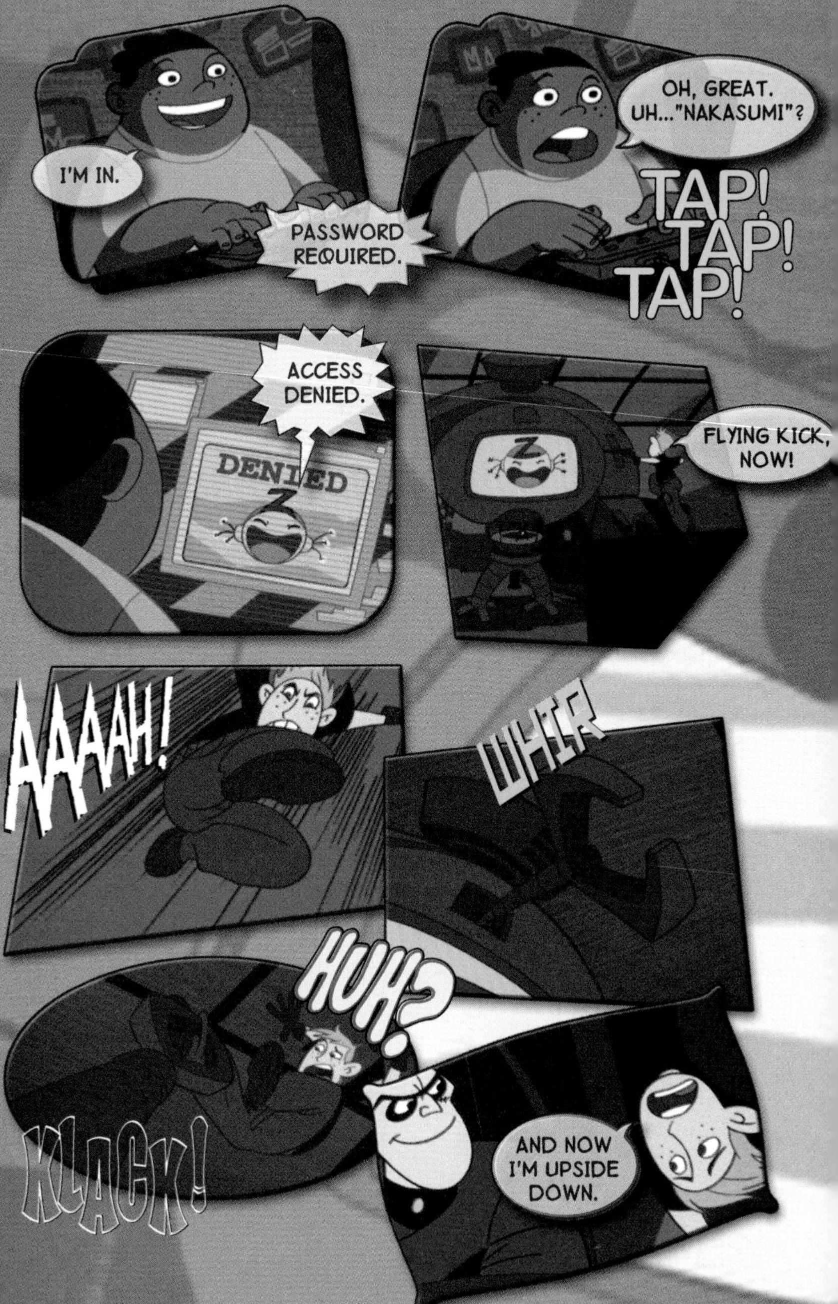
I'M IN.
PASSWORD REQUIRED.
OH, GREAT. UH..."NAKASUMI"?
TAP! TAP! TAP!
ACCESS DENIED.
DENIED
FLYING KICK, NOW!
AAAAH!
WHIR
HUH?
KLACK!
AND NOW I'M UPSIDE DOWN.

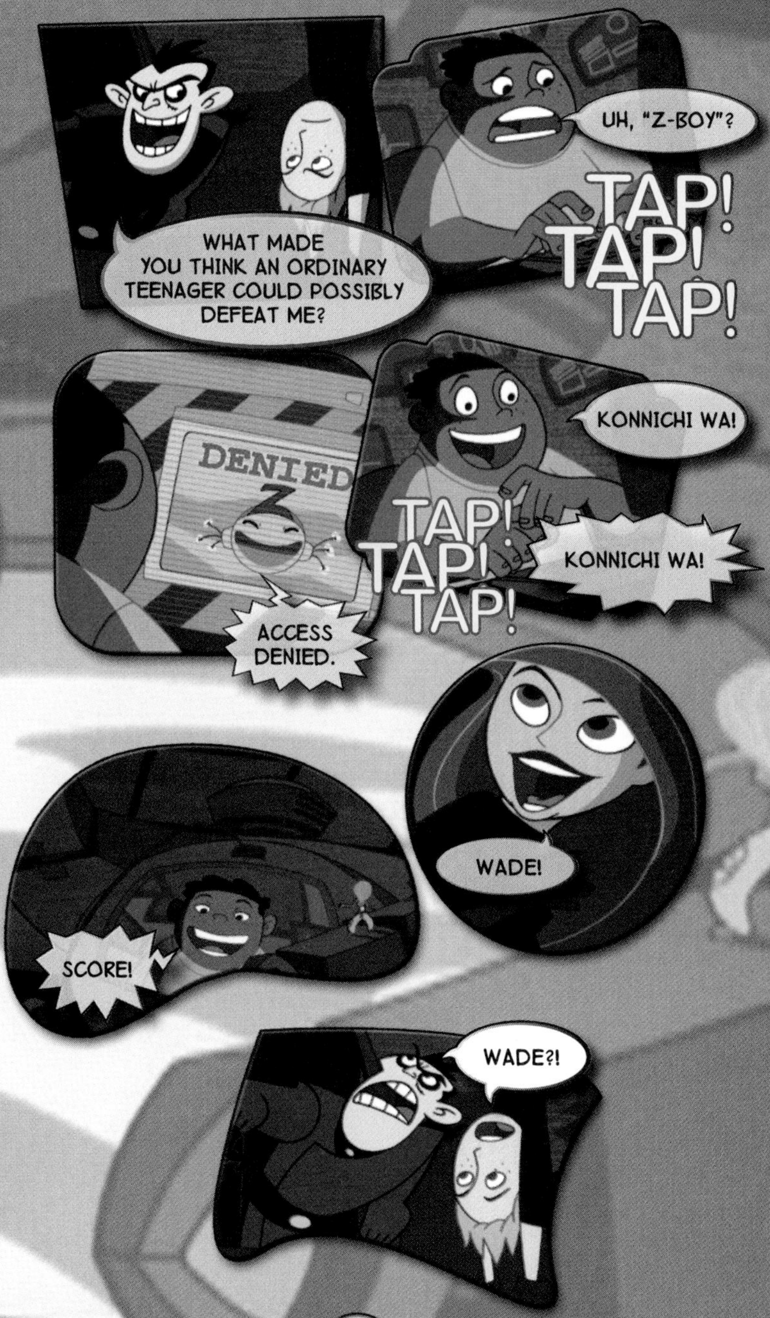
UH, "Z-BOY"?
WHAT MADE YOU THINK AN ORDINARY TEENAGER COULD POSSIBLY DEFEAT ME?
TAP! TAP! TAP!
DENIED
ACCESS DENIED.
KONNICHI WA!
TAP! TAP! TAP!
KONNICHI WA!
WADE!
SCORE!
WADE?!

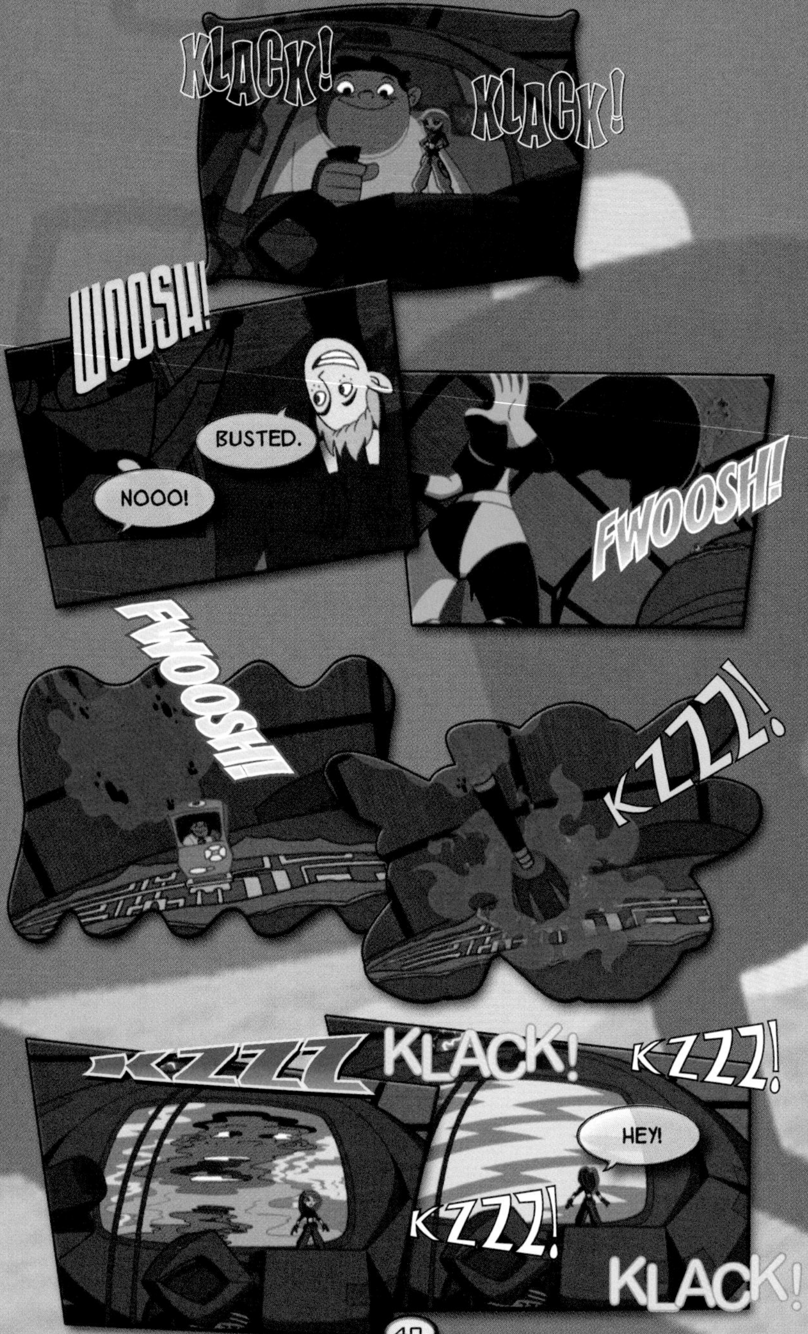
KLACK!
KLACK!
WOOSH!
BUSTED.
NOOO!
FWOOSH!
FWOOSH!
KZZZ!
KZZZ
KLACK!
KZZZ!
HEY!
KZZZ!
KLACK!

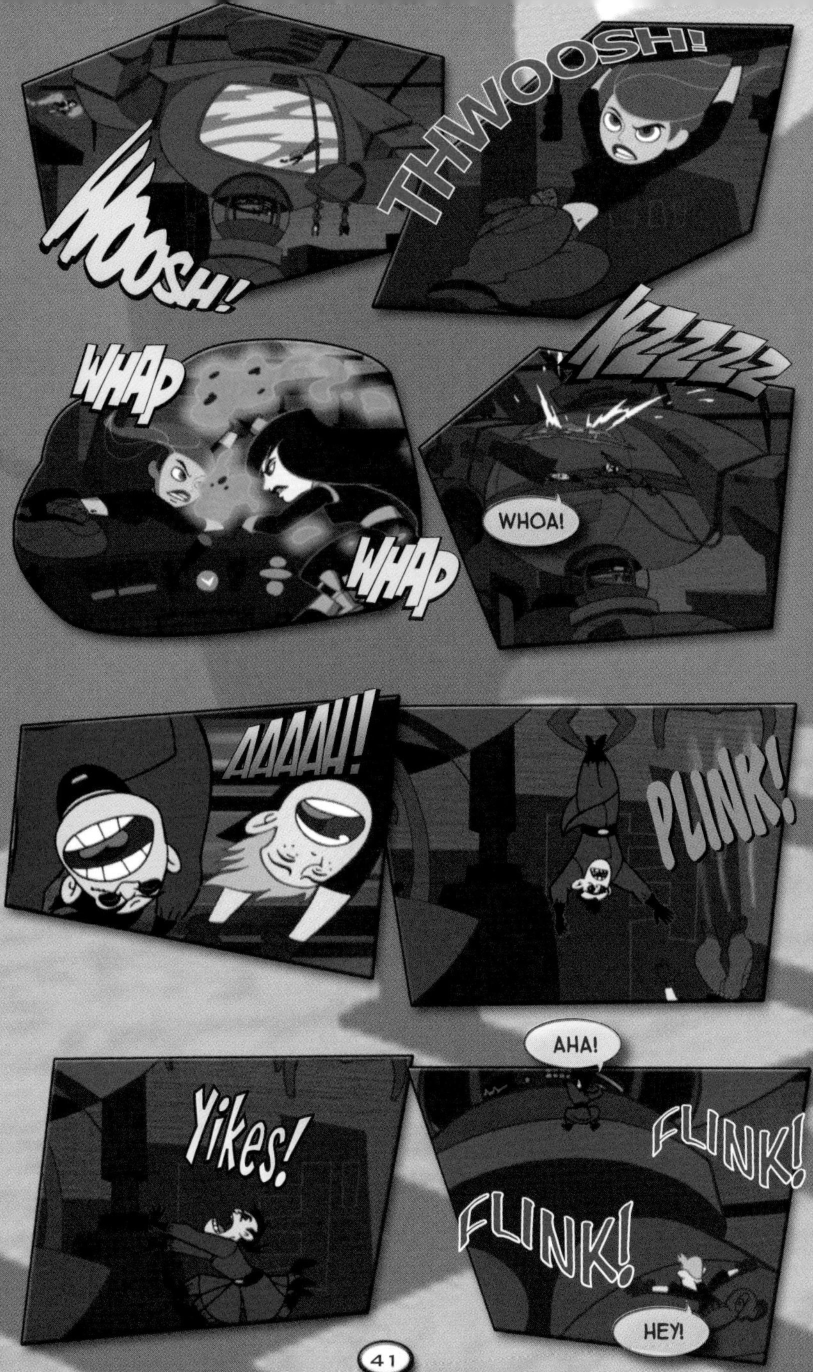
WHOOSH!
THWOOSH!
WHAP
WHAP
KZZZZZ
WHOA!
AAAAH!
PLINK!
Yikes!
AHA!
FLINK!
FLINK!
HEY!

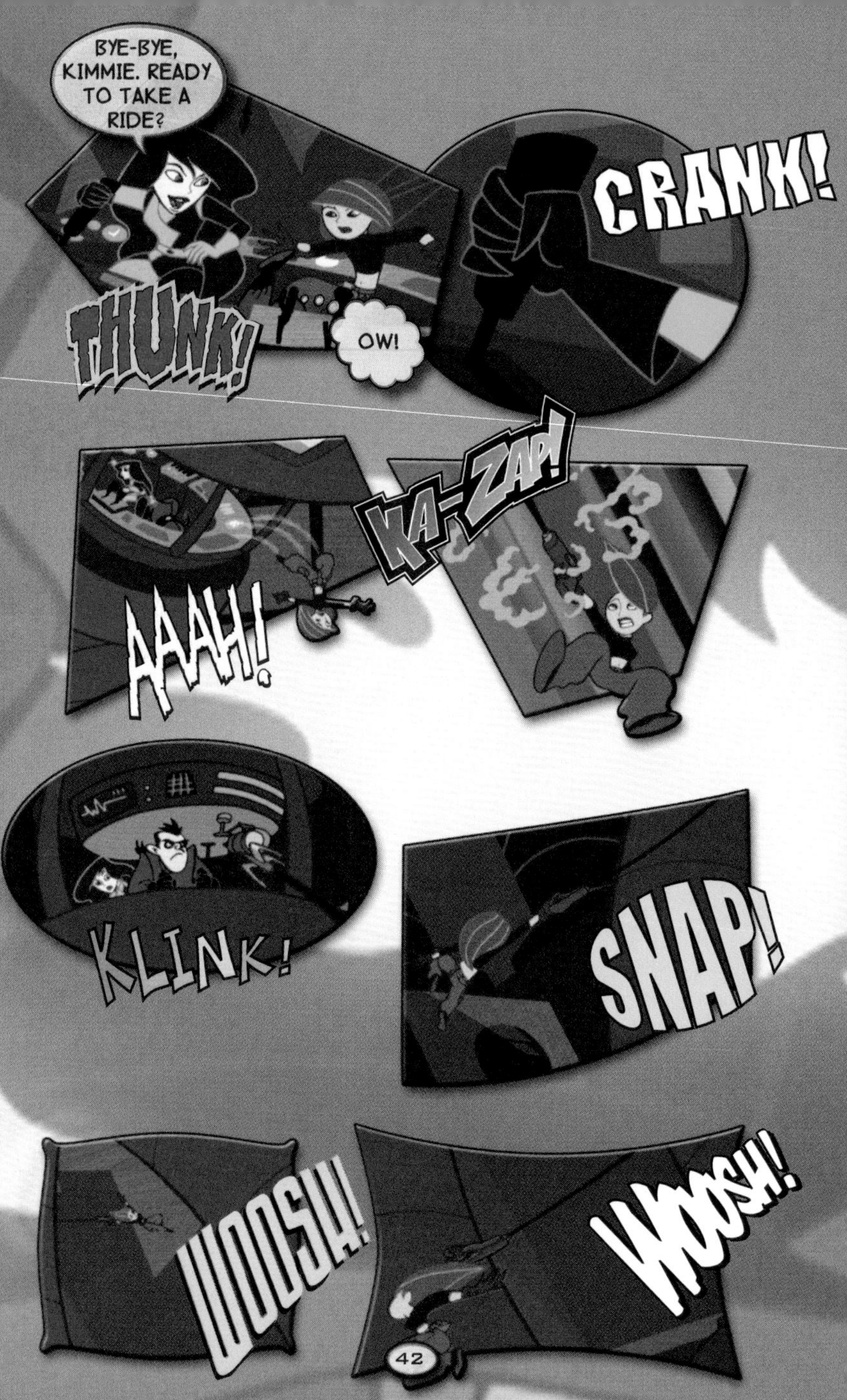
BYE-BYE, KIMMIE. READY TO TAKE A RIDE?
THUNK!
OW!
CRANK!
AAAH!
KA-ZAP!
KLINK!
SNAP!
WOOSH!
WOOSH!

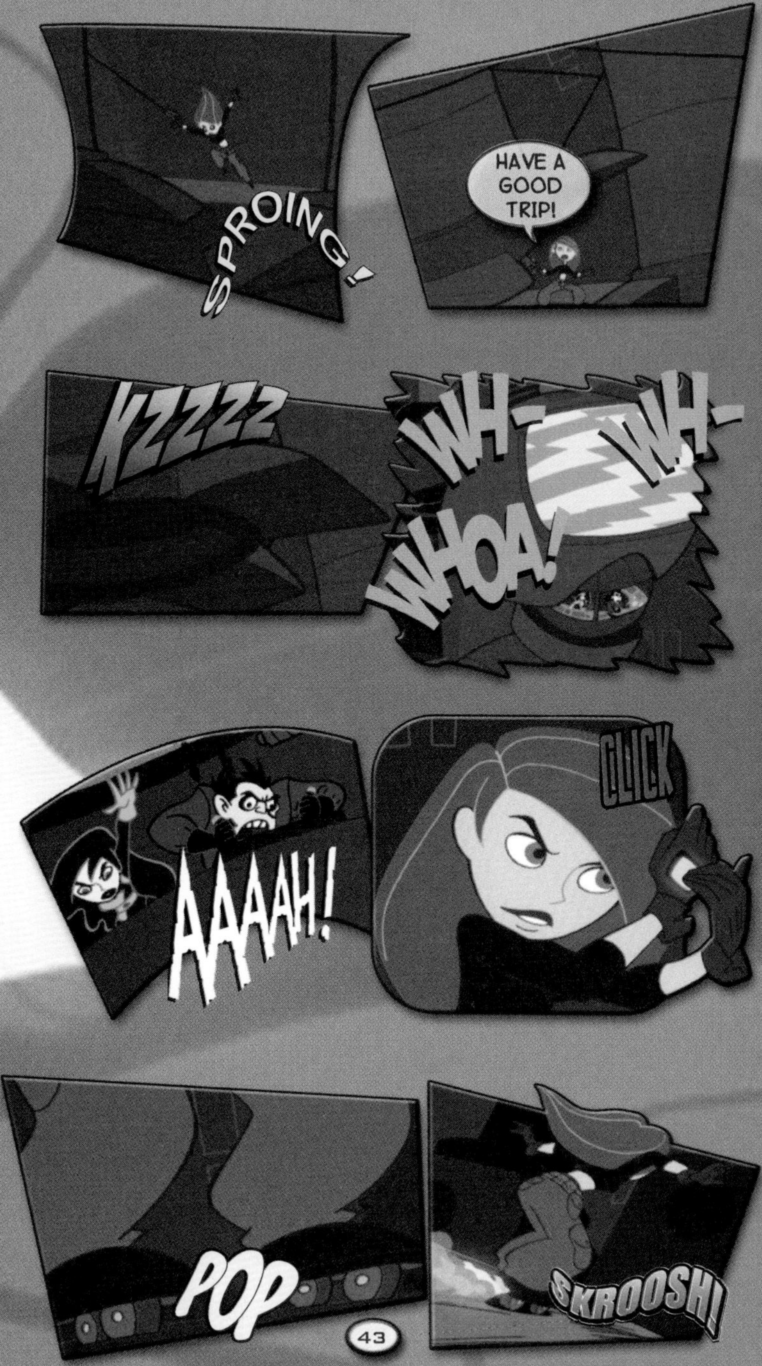
SPROING!
HAVE A
GOOD
TRIP!
KZZZZ
WH-
WH-
WHOA!
AAAAH!
CLICK
POP
SKROOSH!

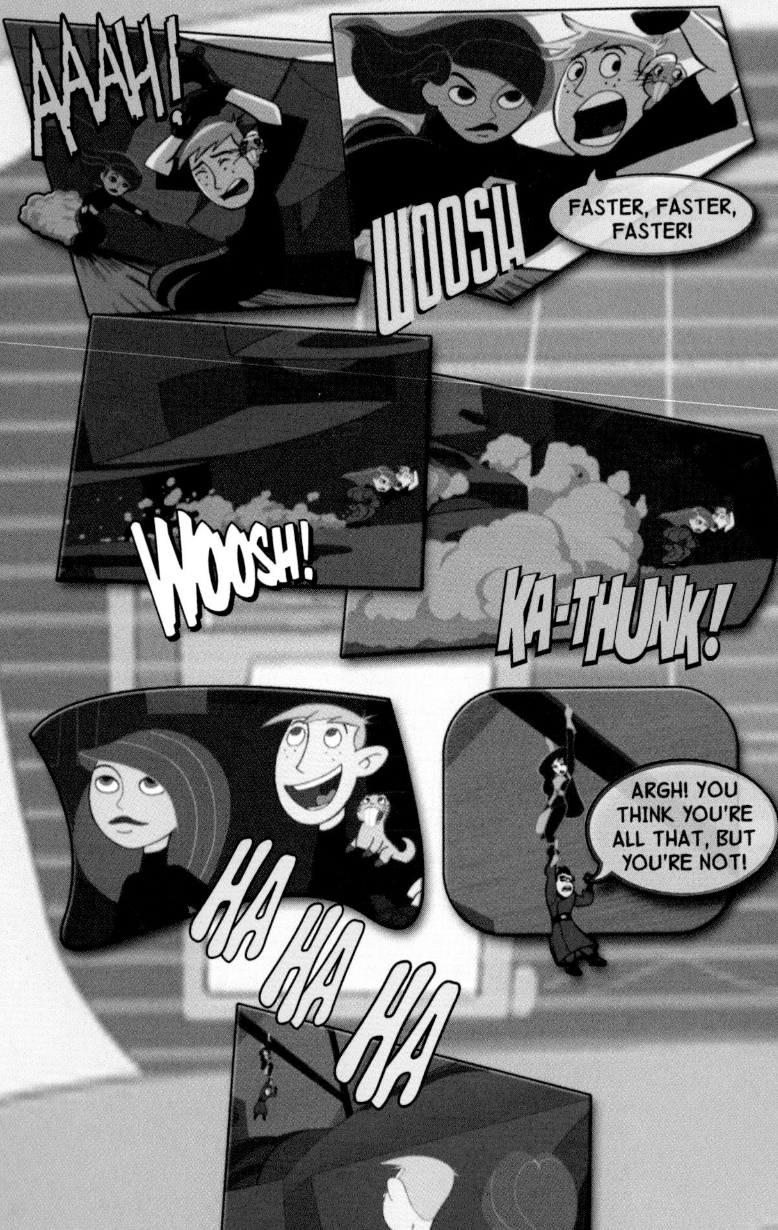
AAAH!
WOOSH
FASTER, FASTER, FASTER!
WOOSH!
KA-THUNK!
HA HA HA HA
ARGH! YOU THINK YOU'RE ALL THAT, BUT YOU'RE NOT!

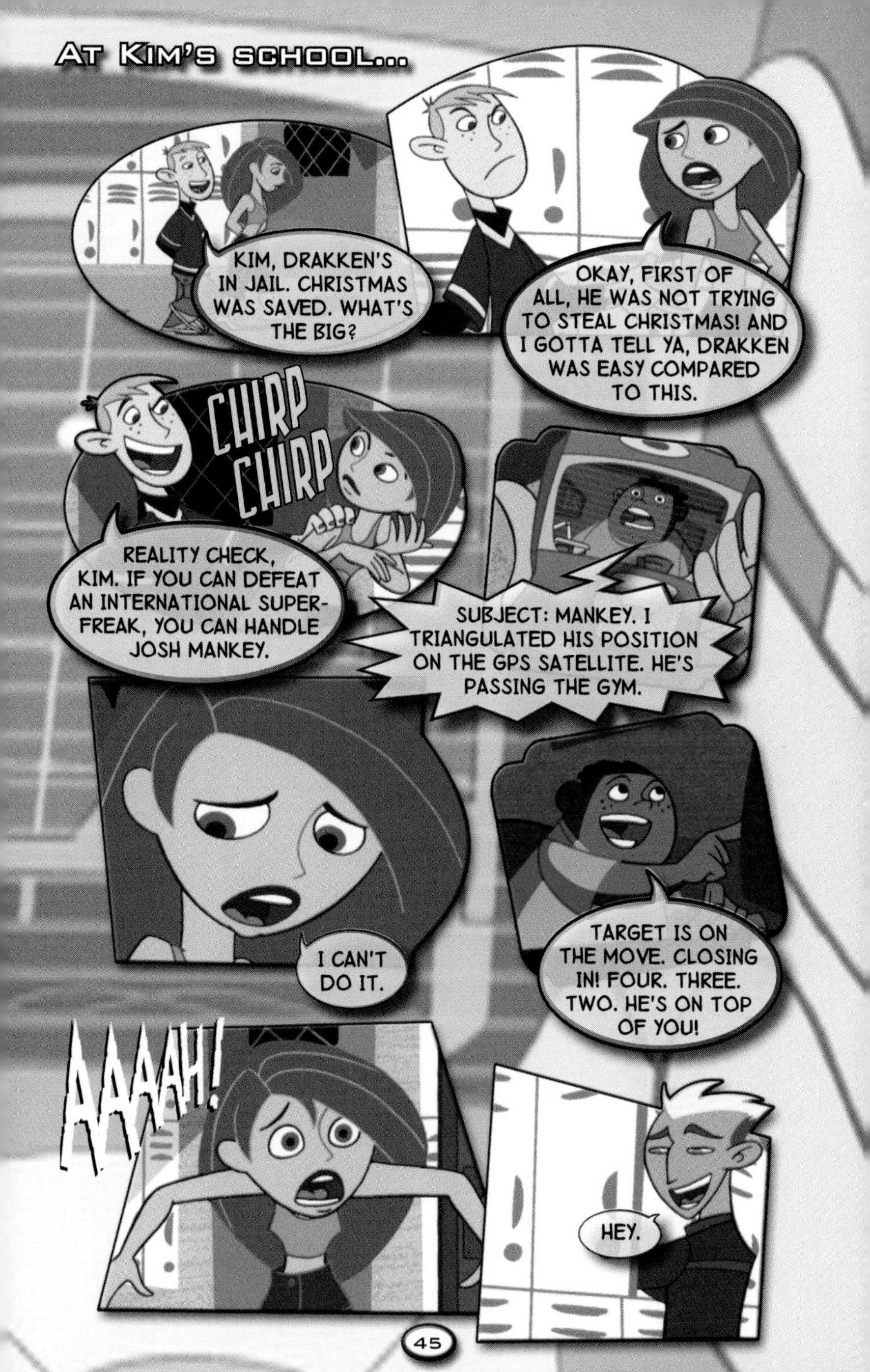

AT KIM'S SCHOOL...
KIM, DRAKKEN'S IN JAIL. CHRISTMAS WAS SAVED. WHAT'S THE BIG?
OKAY, FIRST OF ALL, HE WAS NOT TRYING TO STEAL CHRISTMAS! AND I GOTTA TELL YA, DRAKKEN WAS EASY COMPARED TO THIS.
CHIRP CHIRP
REALITY CHECK, KIM. IF YOU CAN DEFEAT AN INTERNATIONAL SUPER-FREAK, YOU CAN HANDLE JOSH MANKEY.
SUBJECT: MANKEY. I TRIANGULATED HIS POSITION ON THE GPS SATELLITE. HE'S PASSING THE GYM.
I CAN'T DO IT.
TARGET IS ON THE MOVE. CLOSING IN! FOUR. THREE. TWO. HE'S ON TOP OF YOU!
AAAAH!
HEY.

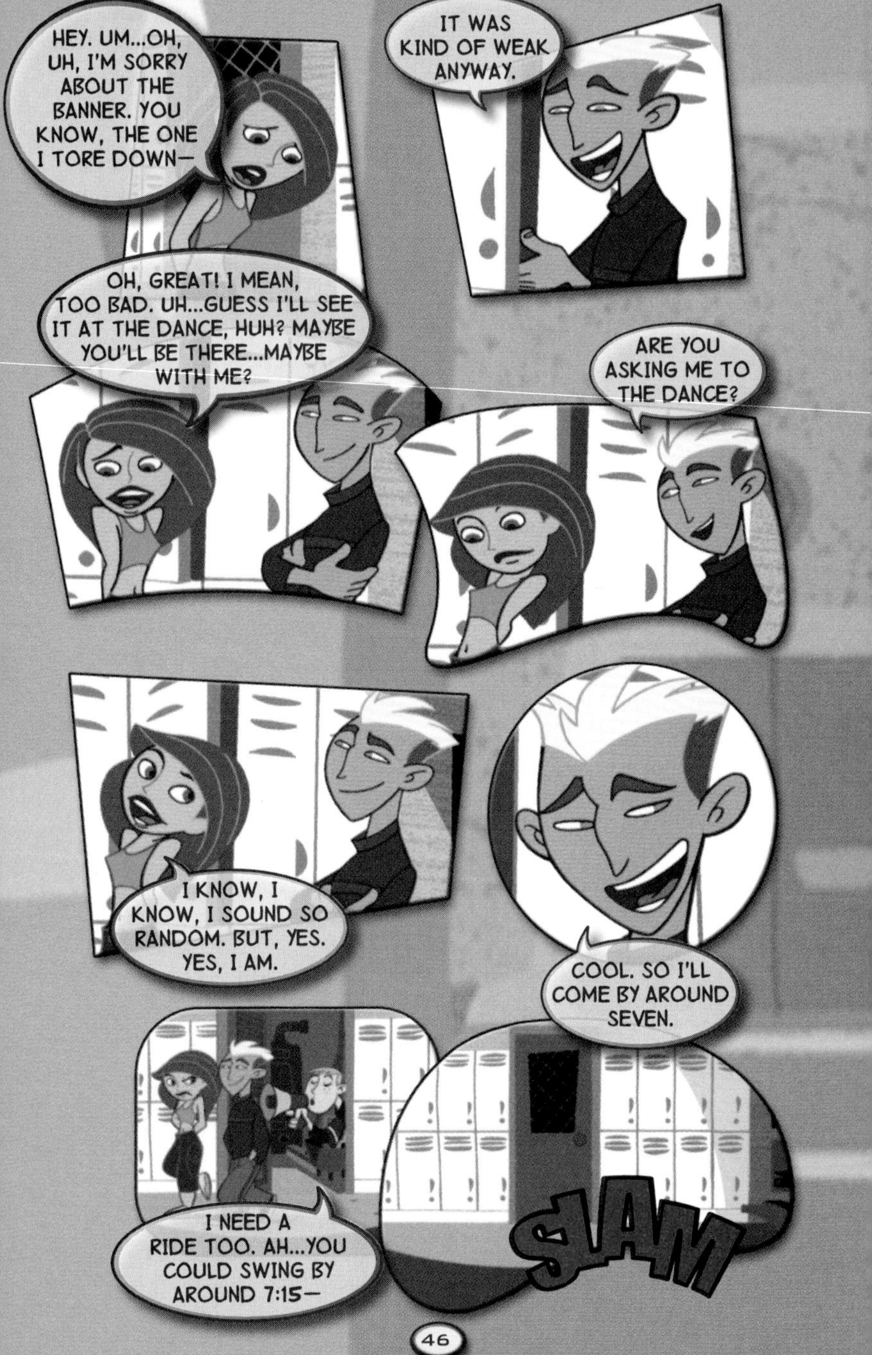
HEY. UM...OH, UH, I'M SORRY ABOUT THE BANNER. YOU KNOW, THE ONE I TORE DOWN—
IT WAS KIND OF WEAK ANYWAY.
OH, GREAT! I MEAN, TOO BAD. UH...GUESS I'LL SEE IT AT THE DANCE, HUH? MAYBE YOU'LL BE THERE...MAYBE WITH ME?
ARE YOU ASKING ME TO THE DANCE?
I KNOW, I KNOW, I SOUND SO RANDOM. BUT, YES. YES, I AM.
COOL. SO I'LL COME BY AROUND SEVEN.
I NEED A RIDE TOO. AH...YOU COULD SWING BY AROUND 7:15—
SLAM

AT THE DANCE...

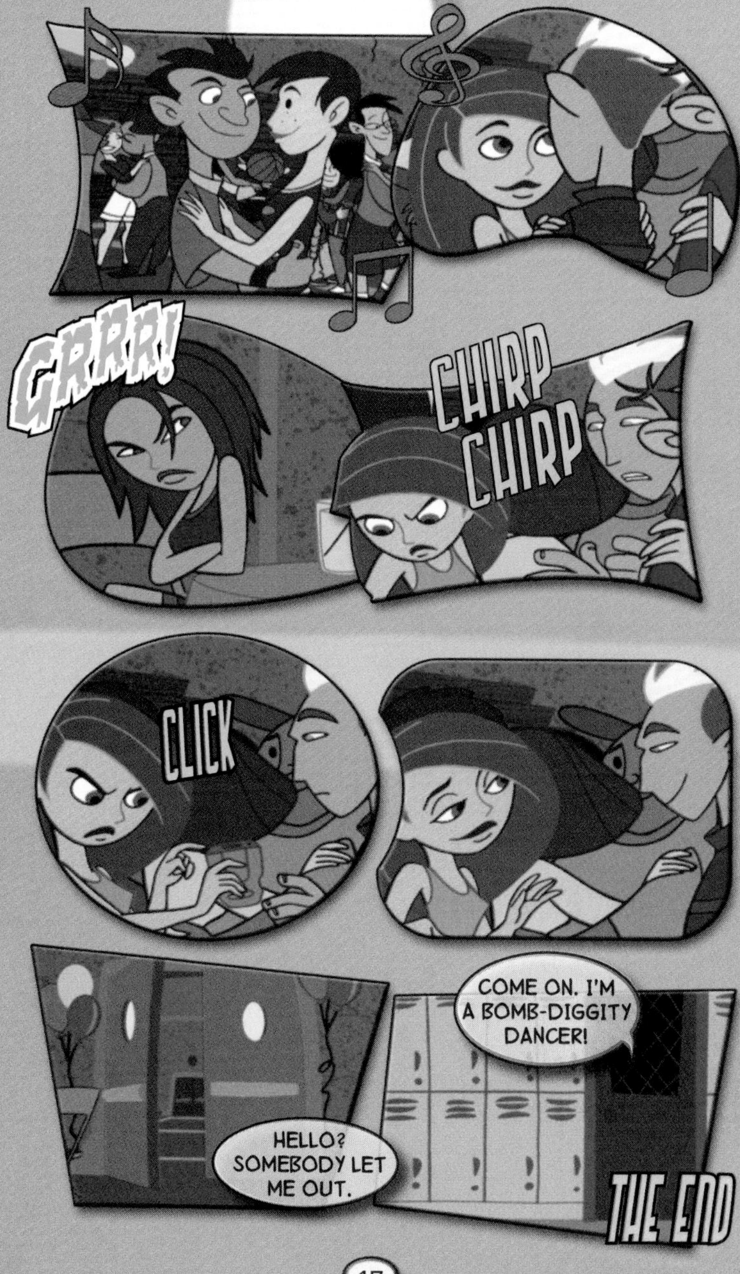
GRRR!
CHIRP CHIRP
CLICK
COME ON. I'M A BOMB-DIGGITY DANCER!
HELLO? SOMEBODY LET ME OUT.
THE END

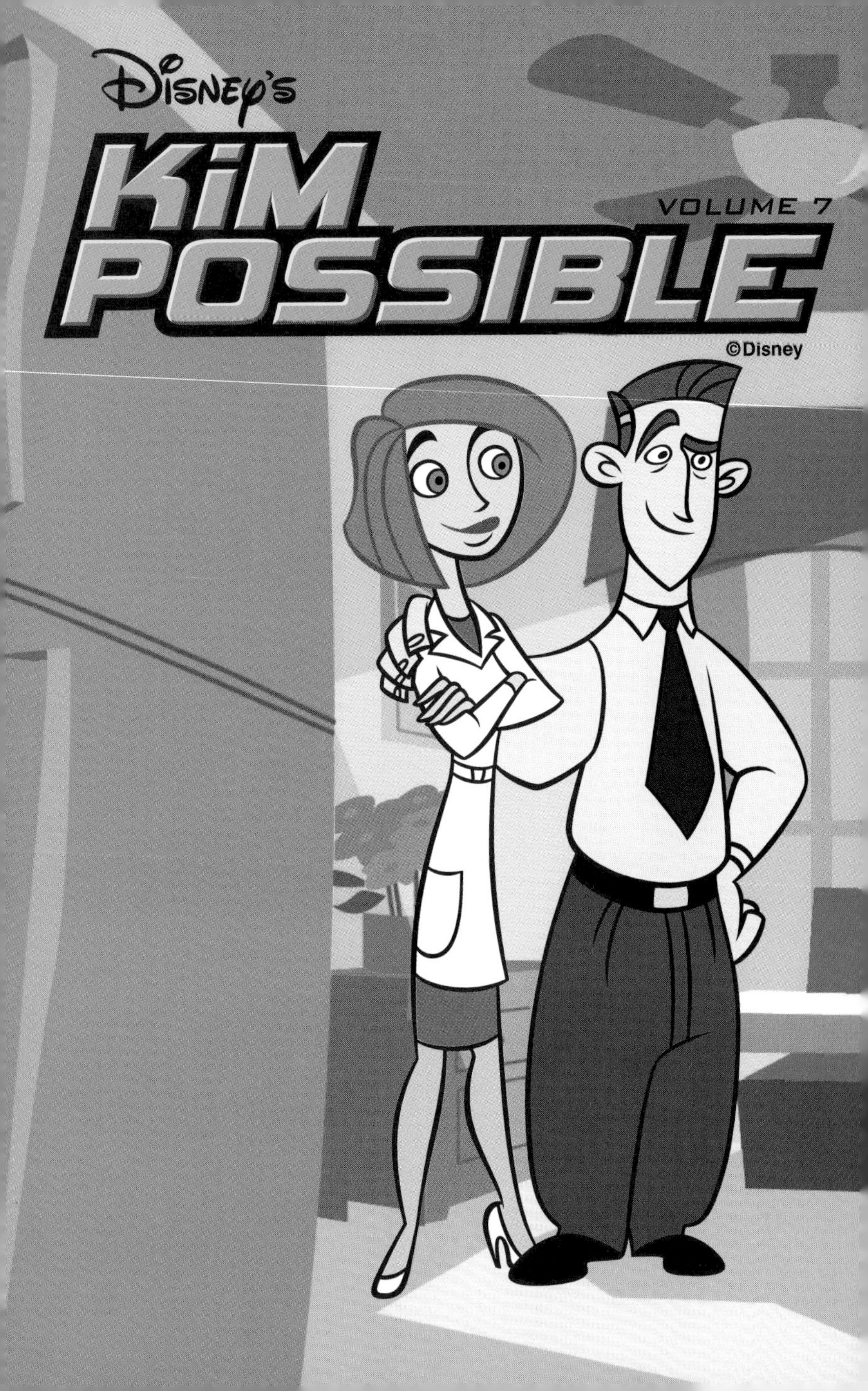
Disney's
Kim Possible
Volume 7
©Disney

Episode 14: Monkey Ninjas in Space

When Monkey Fist tries to fulfill the Monkey Prophecy and become the Ultimate Monkey Master, Kim and Ron are on the case to stop him — with a little help from an unexpected ally.

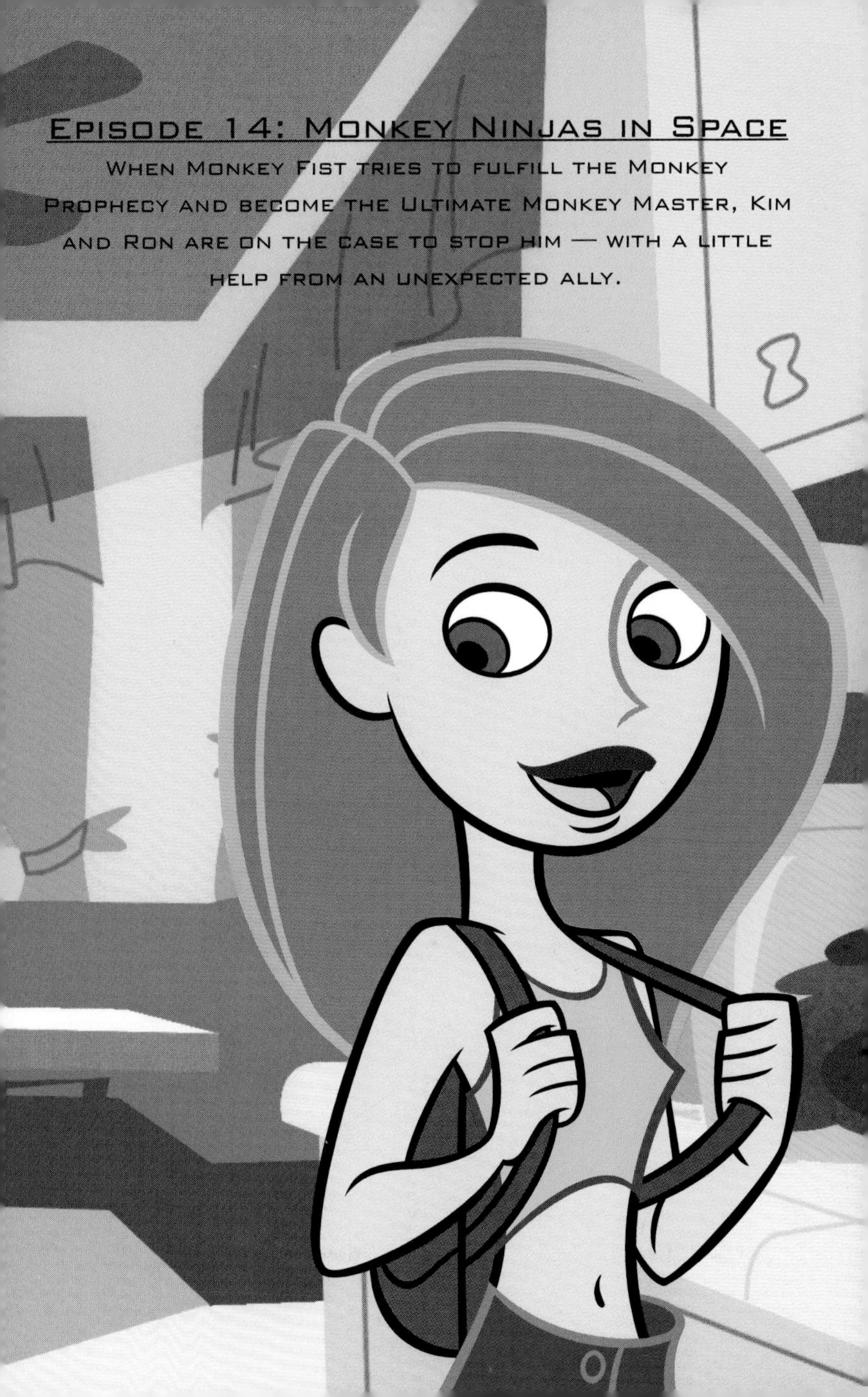

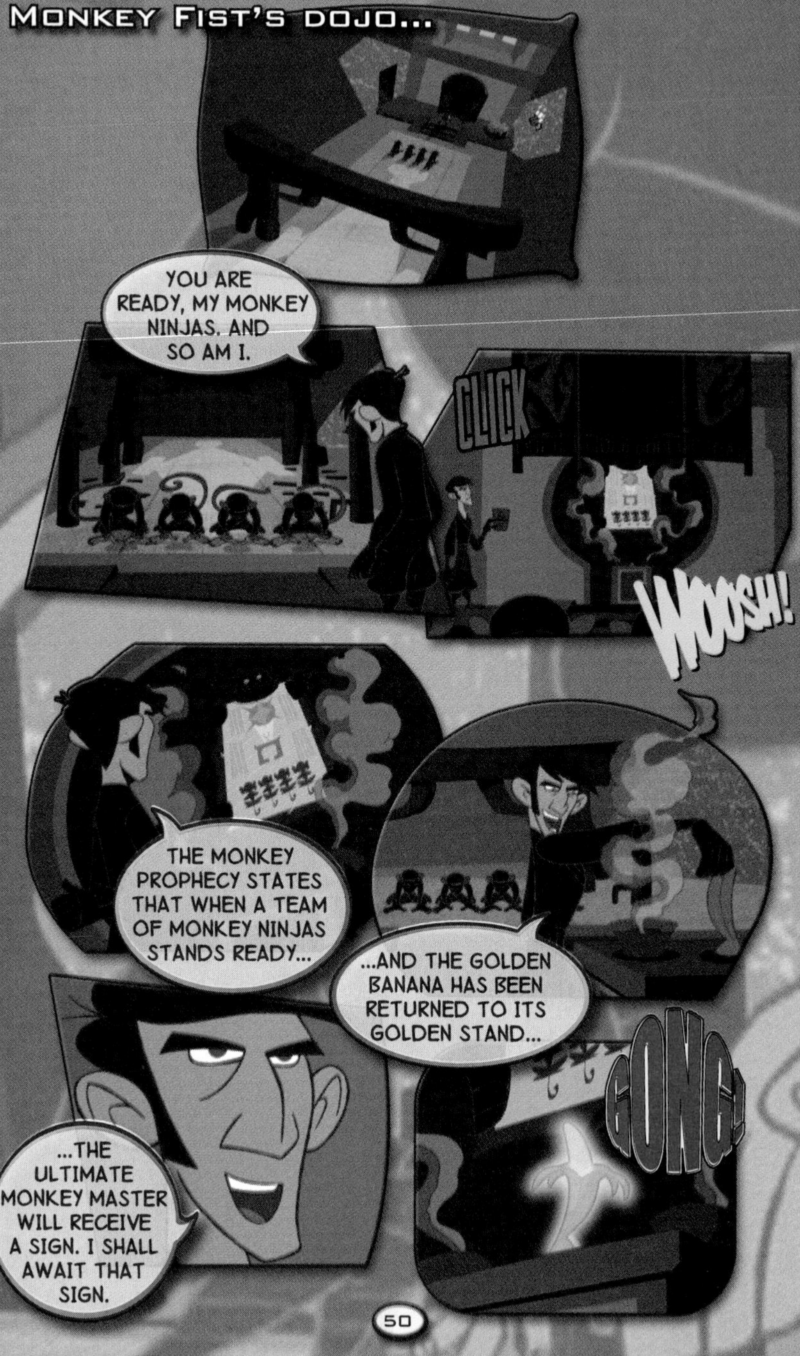

MONKEY FIST'S DOJO...
YOU ARE READY, MY MONKEY NINJAS. AND SO AM I.
CLICK
WOOSH!
THE MONKEY PROPHECY STATES THAT WHEN A TEAM OF MONKEY NINJAS STANDS READY...
...AND THE GOLDEN BANANA HAS BEEN RETURNED TO ITS GOLDEN STAND...
GONG!
...THE ULTIMATE MONKEY MASTER WILL RECEIVE A SIGN. I SHALL AWAIT THAT SIGN.

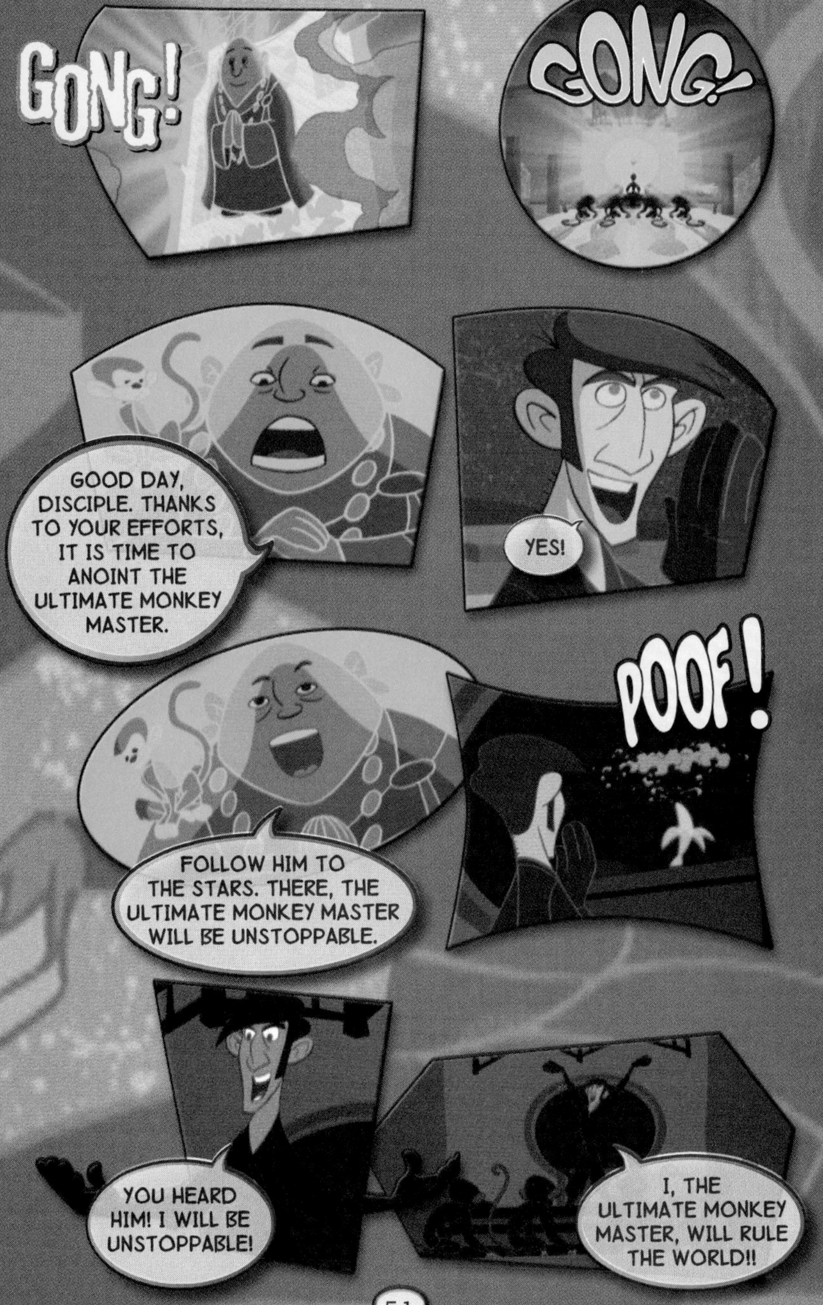
GONG!
GONG!
GOOD DAY, DISCIPLE. THANKS TO YOUR EFFORTS, IT IS TIME TO ANOINT THE ULTIMATE MONKEY MASTER.
YES!
FOLLOW HIM TO THE STARS. THERE, THE ULTIMATE MONKEY MASTER WILL BE UNSTOPPABLE.
POOF!
YOU HEARD HIM! I WILL BE UNSTOPPABLE!
I, THE ULTIMATE MONKEY MASTER, WILL RULE THE WORLD!!

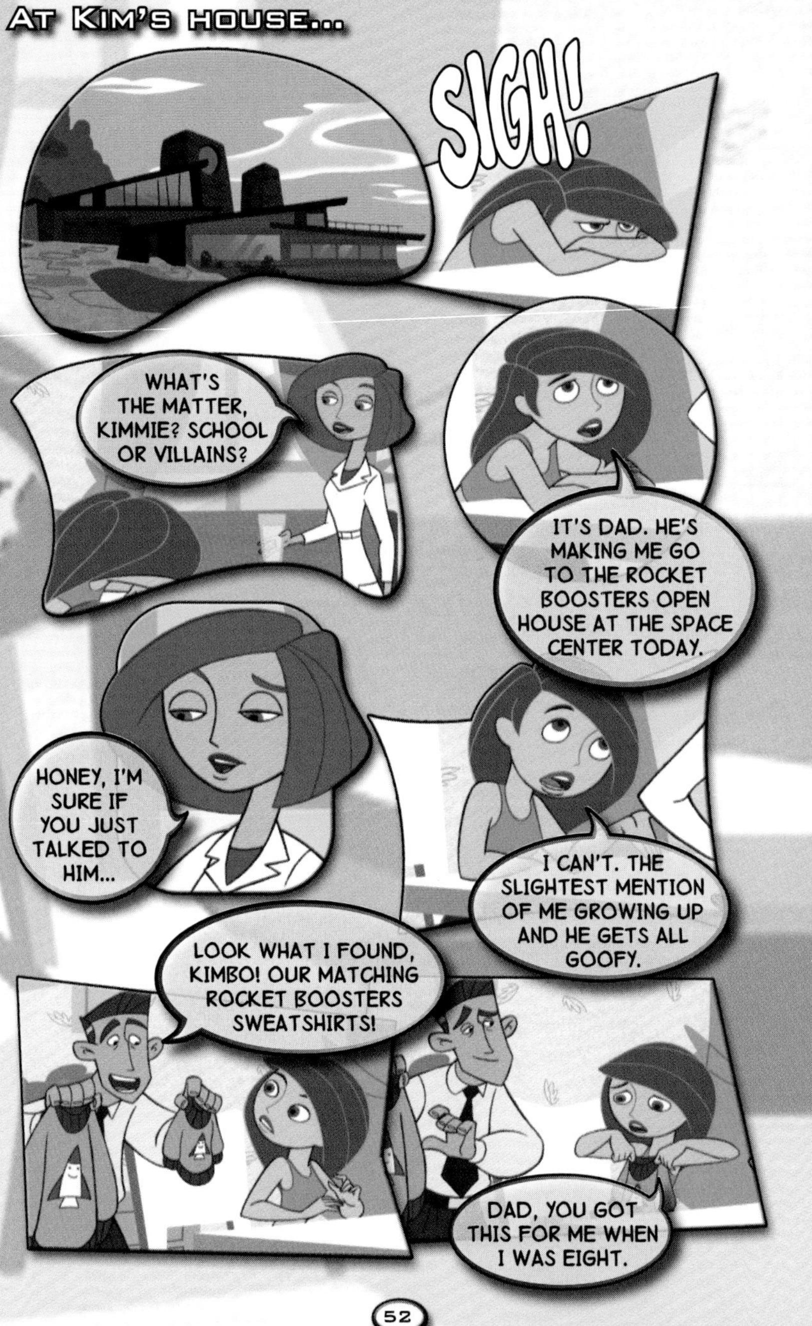
AT KIM'S HOUSE...
SIGH!
WHAT'S THE MATTER, KIMMIE? SCHOOL OR VILLAINS?
IT'S DAD. HE'S MAKING ME GO TO THE ROCKET BOOSTERS OPEN HOUSE AT THE SPACE CENTER TODAY.
HONEY, I'M SURE IF YOU JUST TALKED TO HIM...
I CAN'T. THE SLIGHTEST MENTION OF ME GROWING UP AND HE GETS ALL GOOFY.
LOOK WHAT I FOUND, KIMBO! OUR MATCHING ROCKET BOOSTERS SWEATSHIRTS!
DAD, YOU GOT THIS FOR ME WHEN I WAS EIGHT.

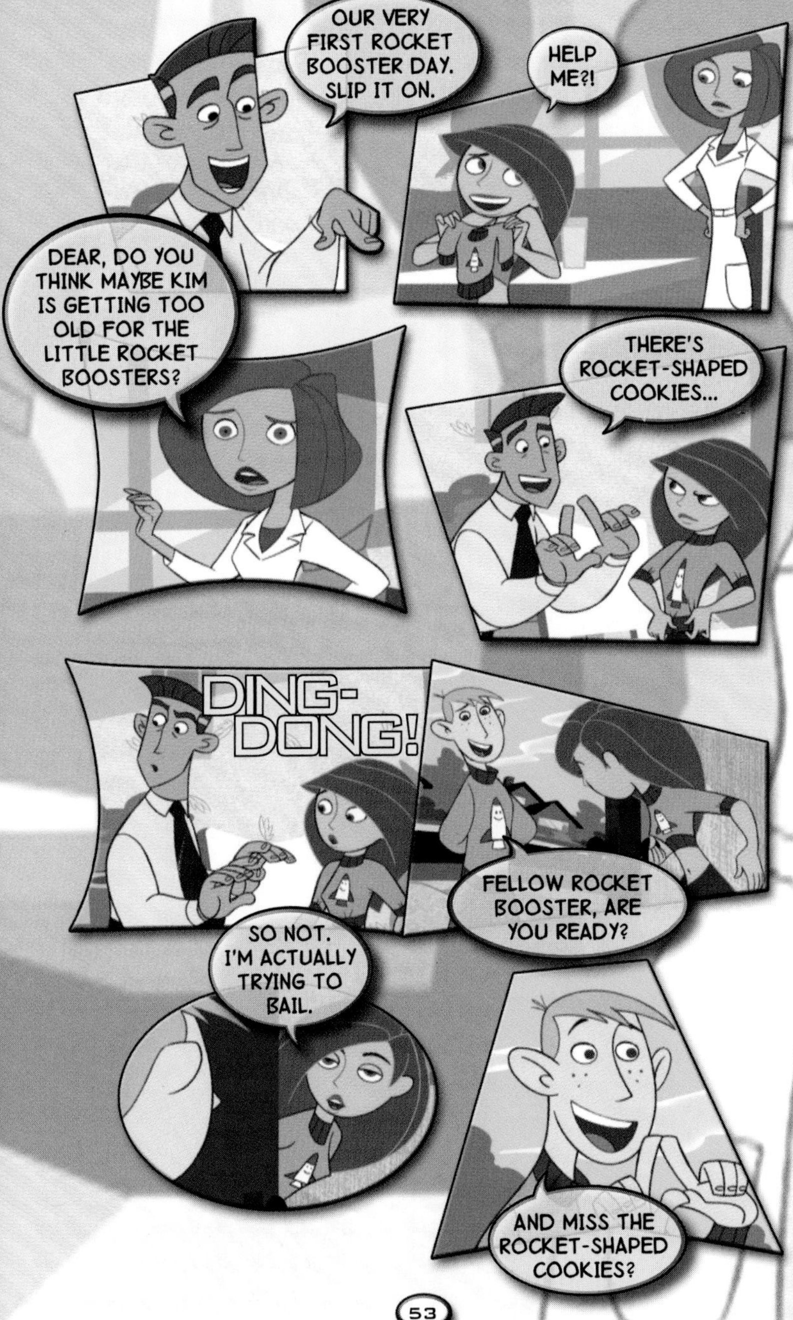
OUR VERY FIRST ROCKET BOOSTER DAY. SLIP IT ON.
HELP ME?!
DEAR, DO YOU THINK MAYBE KIM IS GETTING TOO OLD FOR THE LITTLE ROCKET BOOSTERS?
THERE'S ROCKET-SHAPED COOKIES...
DING-DONG!
FELLOW ROCKET BOOSTER, ARE YOU READY?
SO NOT. I'M ACTUALLY TRYING TO BAIL.
AND MISS THE ROCKET-SHAPED COOKIES?

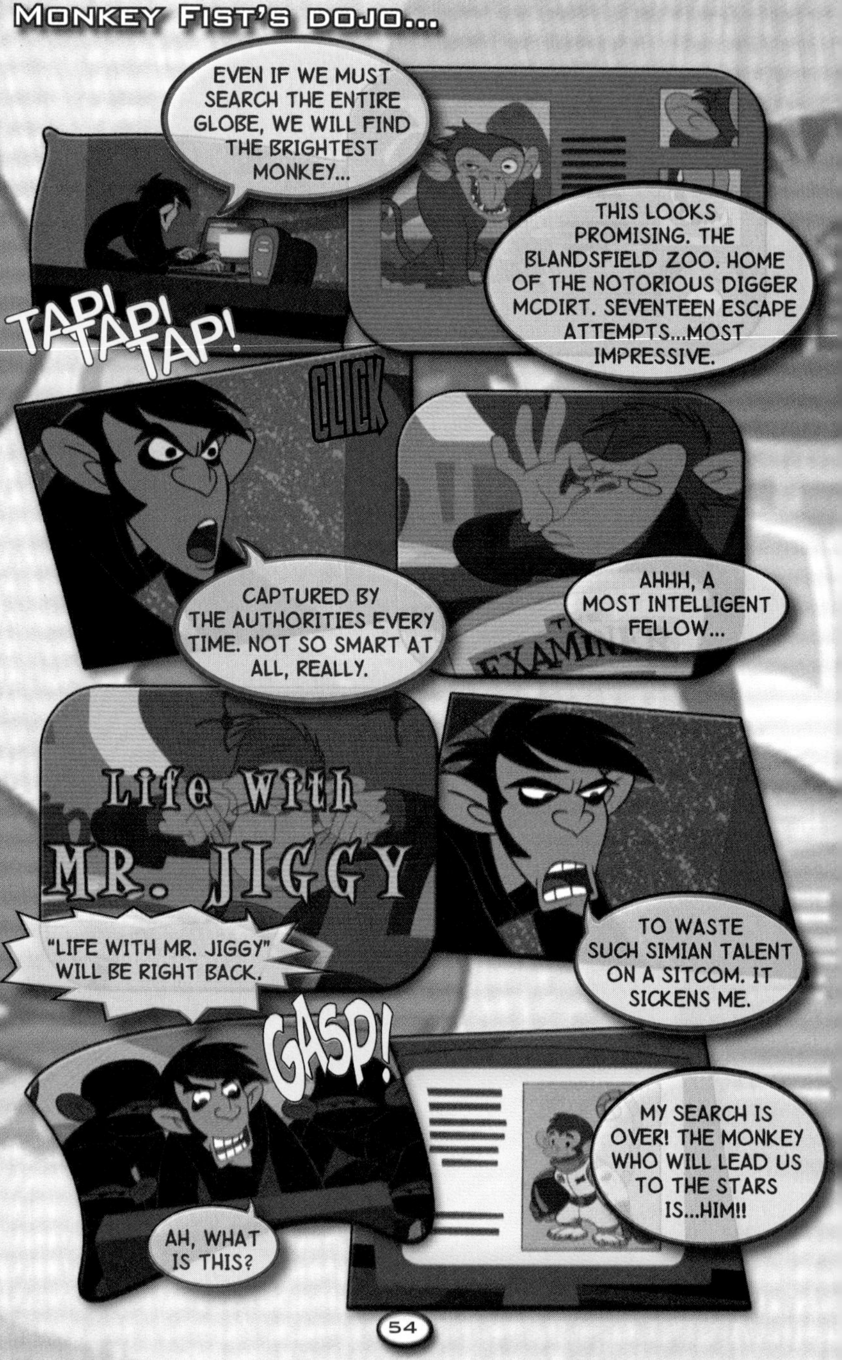
MONKEY FIST'S DOJO...
EVEN IF WE MUST SEARCH THE ENTIRE GLOBE, WE WILL FIND THE BRIGHTEST MONKEY...
TAP! TAP! TAP!
THIS LOOKS PROMISING. THE BLANDSFIELD ZOO. HOME OF THE NOTORIOUS DIGGER MCDIRT. SEVENTEEN ESCAPE ATTEMPTS...MOST IMPRESSIVE.
CLICK
CAPTURED BY THE AUTHORITIES EVERY TIME. NOT SO SMART AT ALL, REALLY.
AHHH, A MOST INTELLIGENT FELLOW...
Life With MR. JIGGY
"LIFE WITH MR. JIGGY" WILL BE RIGHT BACK.
TO WASTE SUCH SIMIAN TALENT ON A SITCOM. IT SICKENS ME.
GASP!
AH, WHAT IS THIS?
MY SEARCH IS OVER! THE MONKEY WHO WILL LEAD US TO THE STARS IS...HIM!!

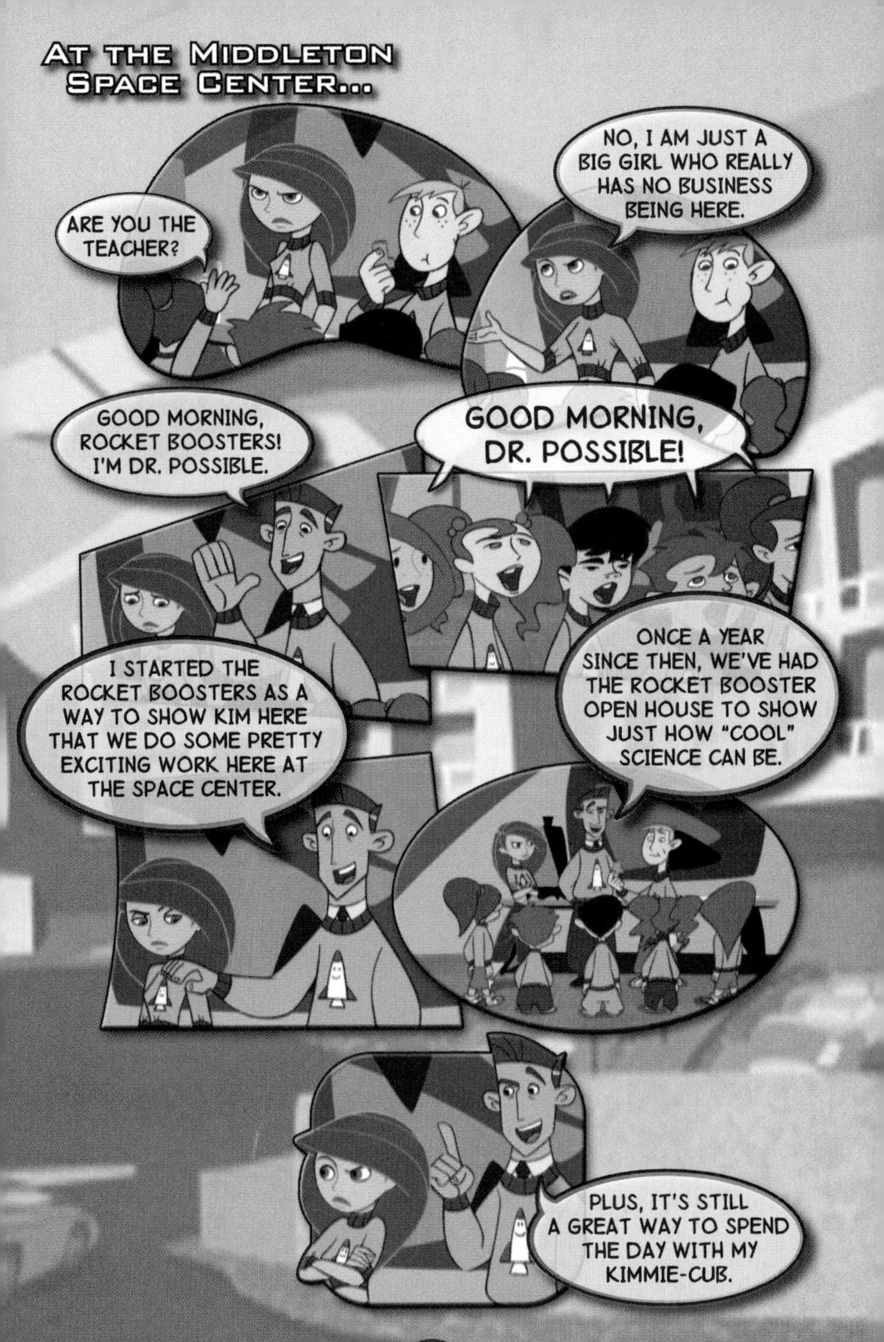
AT THE MIDDLETON SPACE CENTER...
ARE YOU THE TEACHER?
NO, I AM JUST A BIG GIRL WHO REALLY HAS NO BUSINESS BEING HERE.
GOOD MORNING, ROCKET BOOSTERS! I'M DR. POSSIBLE.
GOOD MORNING, DR. POSSIBLE!
I STARTED THE ROCKET BOOSTERS AS A WAY TO SHOW KIM HERE THAT WE DO SOME PRETTY EXCITING WORK HERE AT THE SPACE CENTER.
ONCE A YEAR SINCE THEN, WE'VE HAD THE ROCKET BOOSTER OPEN HOUSE TO SHOW JUST HOW "COOL" SCIENCE CAN BE.
PLUS, IT'S STILL A GREAT WAY TO SPEND THE DAY WITH MY KIMMIE-CUB.

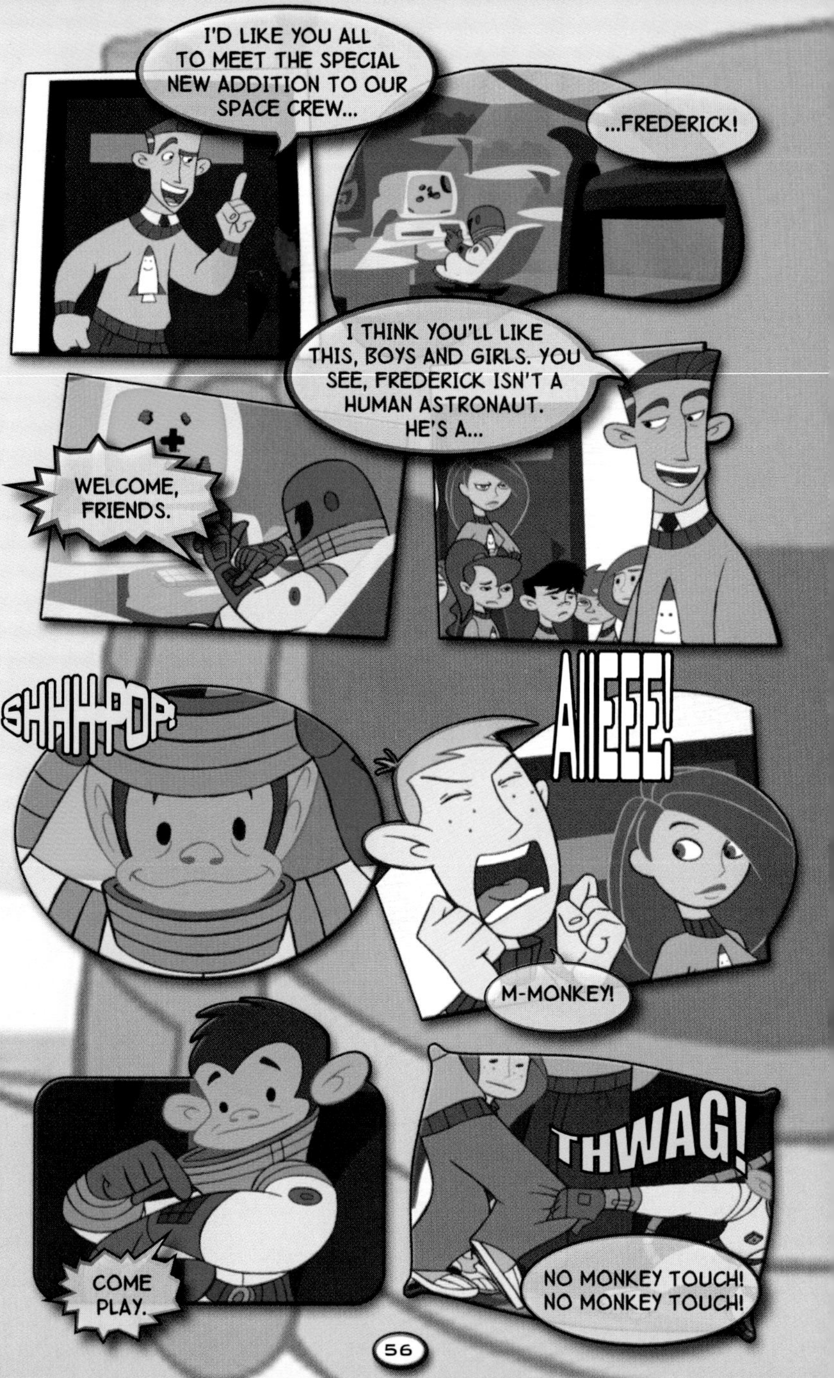
I'D LIKE YOU ALL TO MEET THE SPECIAL NEW ADDITION TO OUR SPACE CREW...
...FREDERICK!
I THINK YOU'LL LIKE THIS, BOYS AND GIRLS. YOU SEE, FREDERICK ISN'T A HUMAN ASTRONAUT. HE'S A...
WELCOME, FRIENDS.
SHHHPOP!
AIIEEE!
M-MONKEY!
COME PLAY.
THWAG!
NO MONKEY TOUCH! NO MONKEY TOUCH!

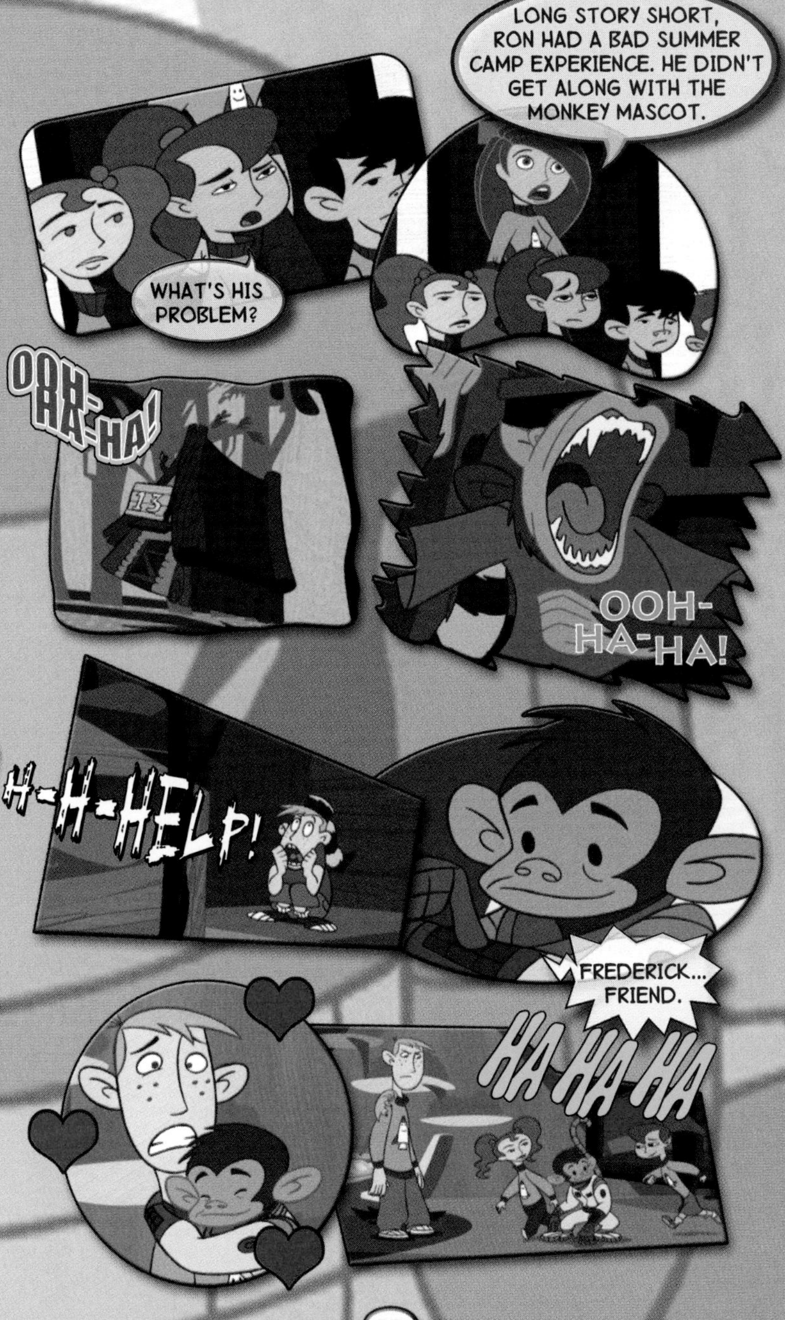
WHAT'S HIS PROBLEM?
LONG STORY SHORT, RON HAD A BAD SUMMER CAMP EXPERIENCE. HE DIDN'T GET ALONG WITH THE MONKEY MASCOT.
OOH-HA-HA!
13
OOH-HA-HA!
H-H-HELP!
FREDERICK... FRIEND.
HA HA HA

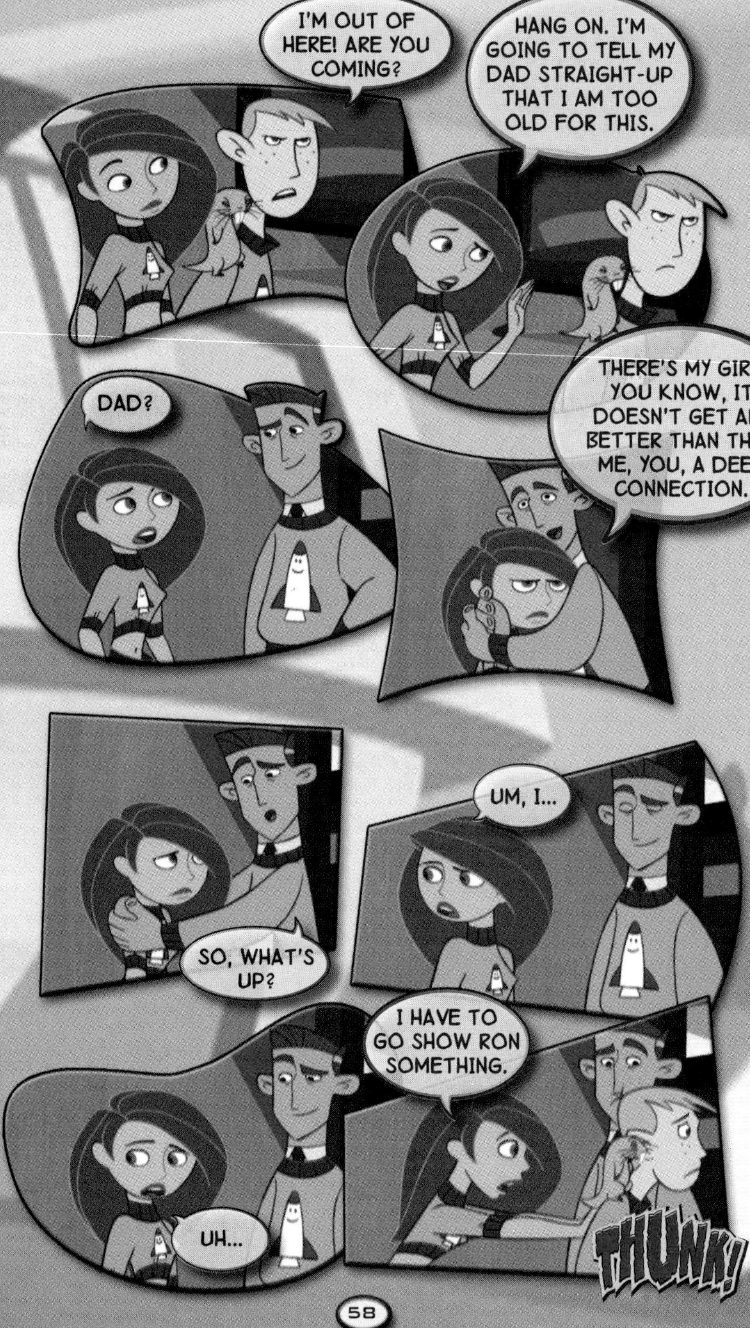
I'M OUT OF HERE! ARE YOU COMING?
HANG ON. I'M GOING TO TELL MY DAD STRAIGHT-UP THAT I AM TOO OLD FOR THIS.
DAD?
THERE'S MY GIRL! YOU KNOW, IT DOESN'T GET ANY BETTER THAN THIS. ME, YOU, A DEEP CONNECTION.
SO, WHAT'S UP?
UM, I...
UH...
I HAVE TO GO SHOW RON SOMETHING.
THUNK!

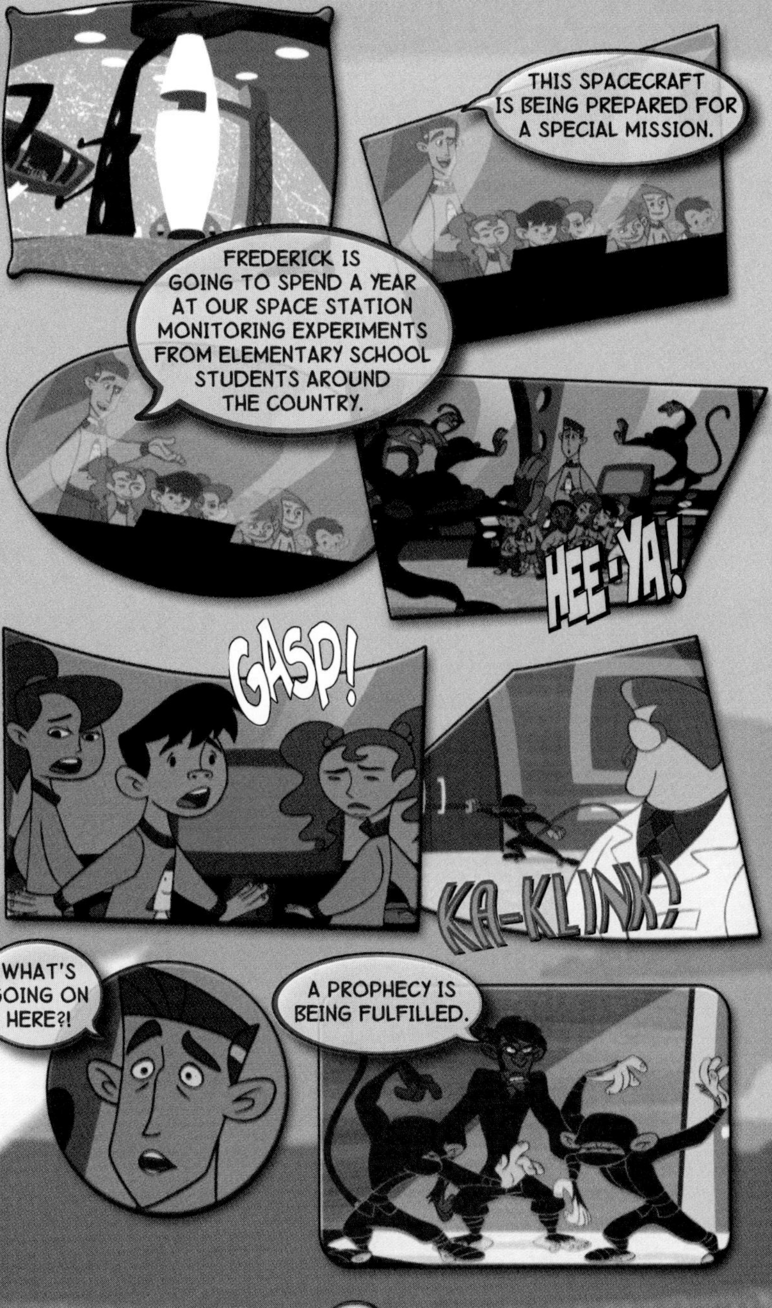

THIS SPACECRAFT IS BEING PREPARED FOR A SPECIAL MISSION.
FREDERICK IS GOING TO SPEND A YEAR AT OUR SPACE STATION MONITORING EXPERIMENTS FROM ELEMENTARY SCHOOL STUDENTS AROUND THE COUNTRY.
HEE-YA!
GASP!
KA-KLINK!
WHAT'S GOING ON HERE?!
A PROPHECY IS BEING FULFILLED.

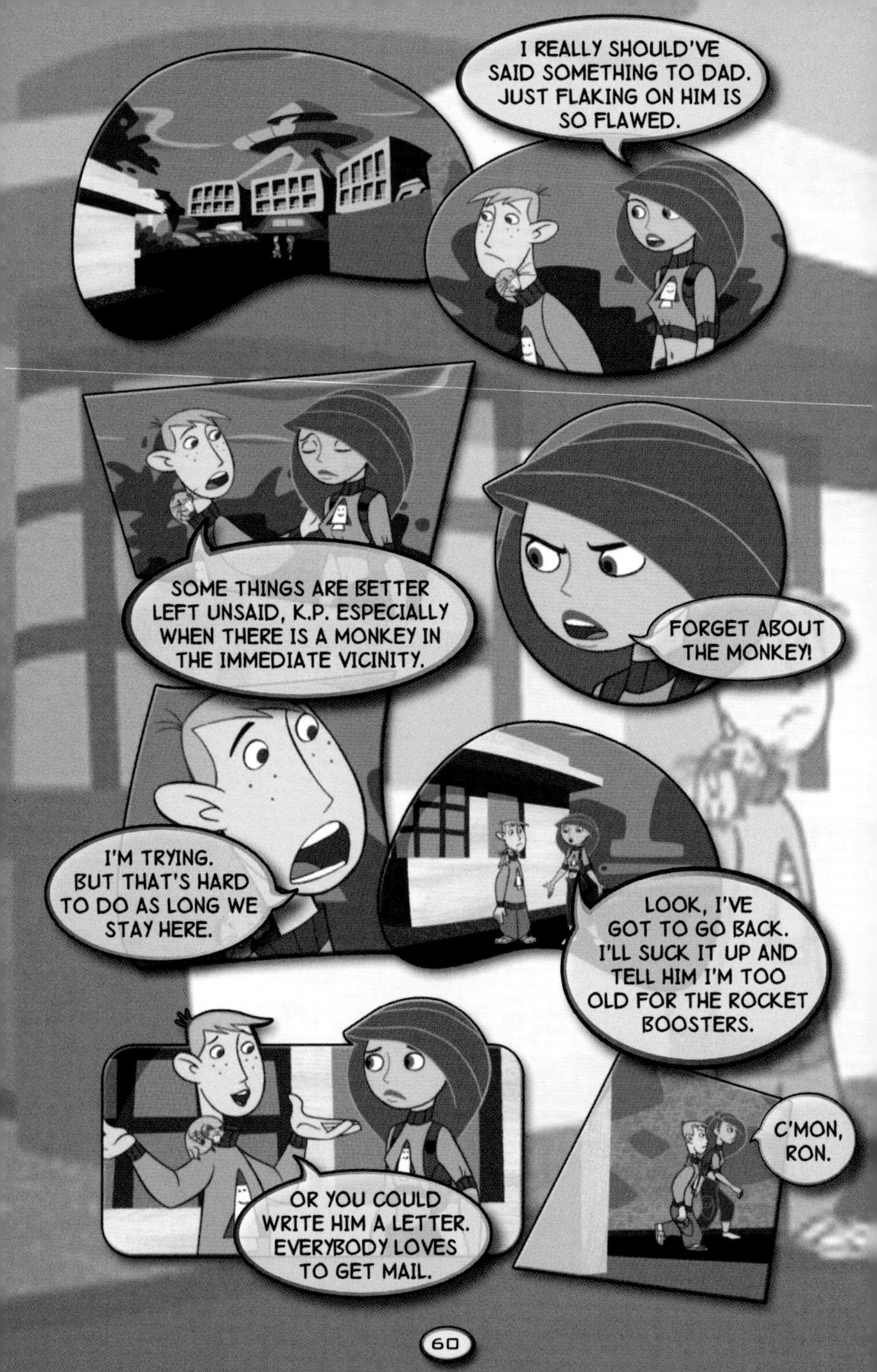
I REALLY SHOULD'VE SAID SOMETHING TO DAD. JUST FLAKING ON HIM IS SO FLAWED.
SOME THINGS ARE BETTER LEFT UNSAID, K.P. ESPECIALLY WHEN THERE IS A MONKEY IN THE IMMEDIATE VICINITY.
FORGET ABOUT THE MONKEY!
I'M TRYING. BUT THAT'S HARD TO DO AS LONG WE STAY HERE.
LOOK, I'VE GOT TO GO BACK. I'LL SUCK IT UP AND TELL HIM I'M TOO OLD FOR THE ROCKET BOOSTERS.
OR YOU COULD WRITE HIM A LETTER. EVERYBODY LOVES TO GET MAIL.
C'MON, RON.

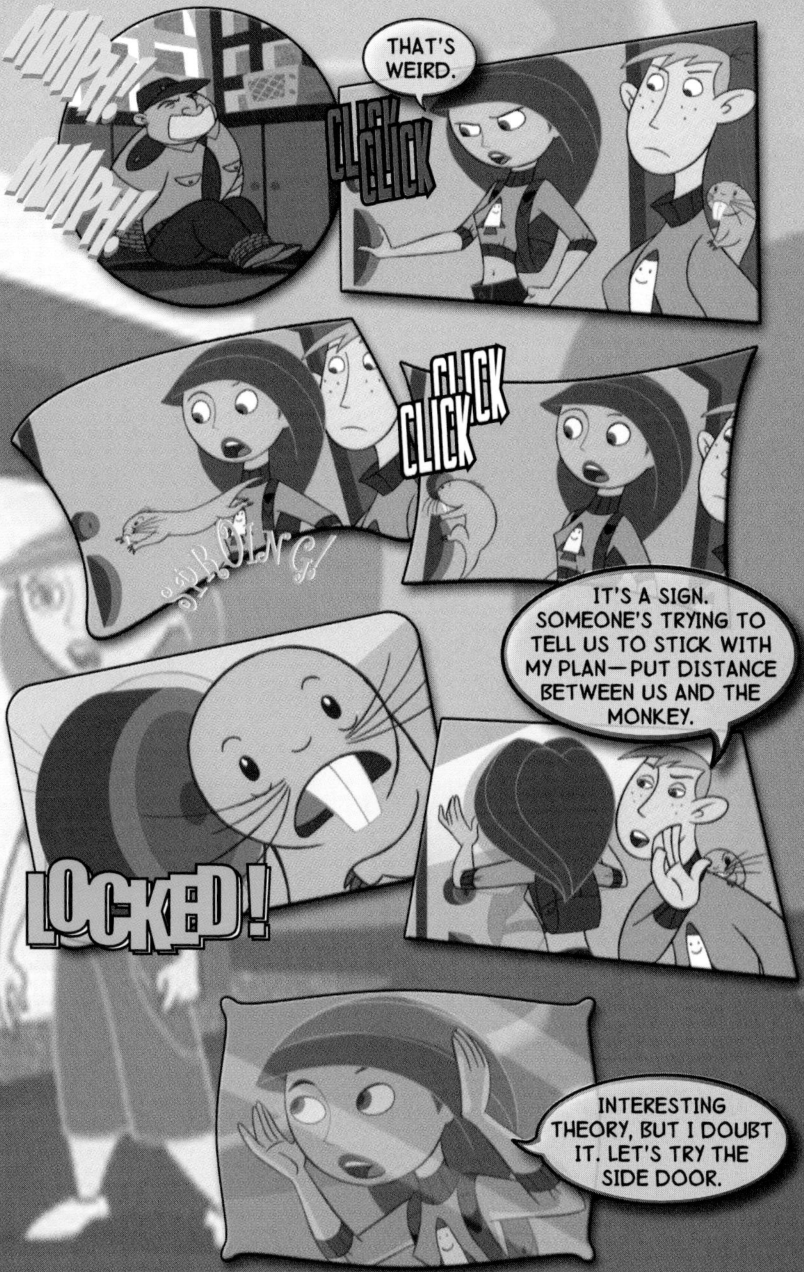
MMPH!! MMPH!!
THAT'S WEIRD.
CLICK CLICK
CLICK CLICK
SPROING!
LOCKED!
IT'S A SIGN. SOMEONE'S TRYING TO TELL US TO STICK WITH MY PLAN—PUT DISTANCE BETWEEN US AND THE MONKEY.
INTERESTING THEORY, BUT I DOUBT IT. LET'S TRY THE SIDE DOOR.

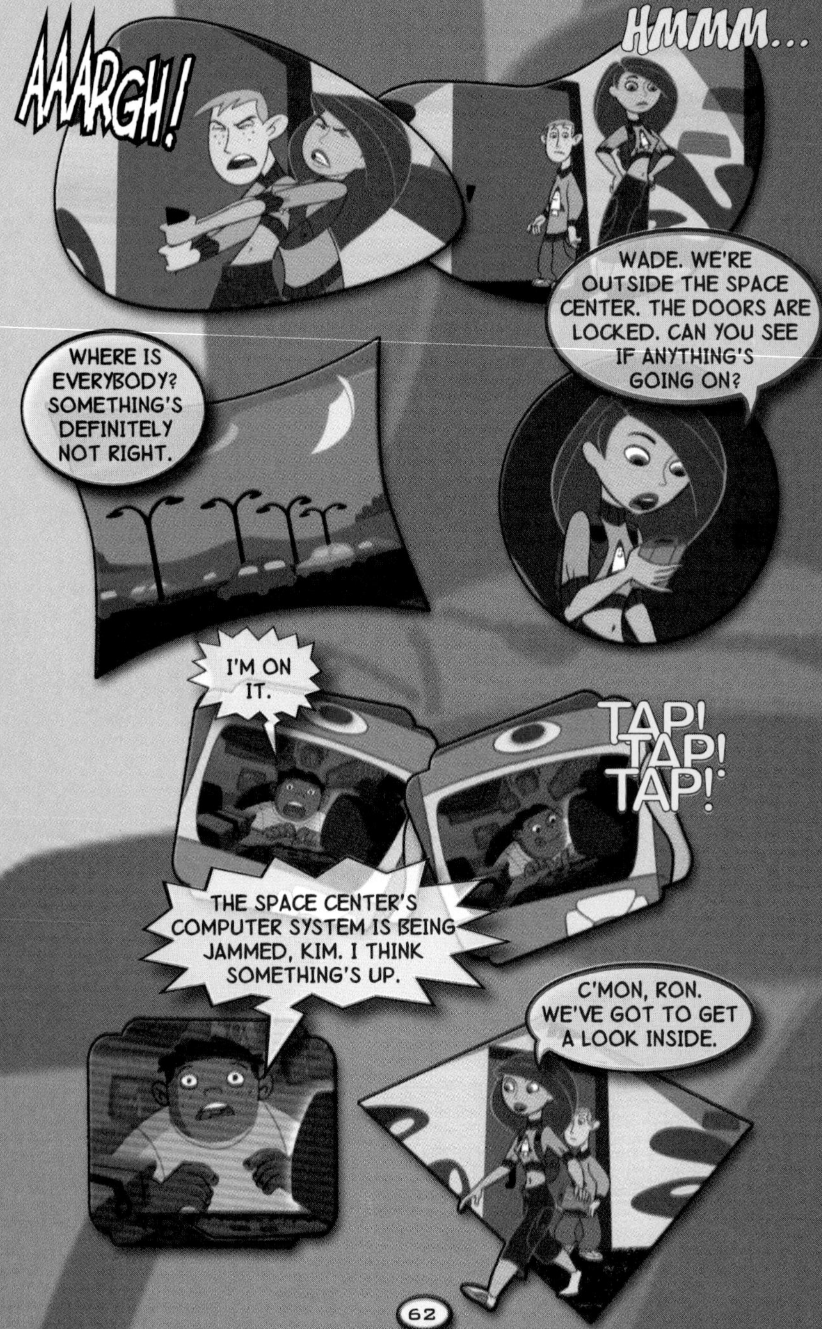
AAARGH!
HMMM...
WADE. WE'RE OUTSIDE THE SPACE CENTER. THE DOORS ARE LOCKED. CAN YOU SEE IF ANYTHING'S GOING ON?
WHERE IS EVERYBODY? SOMETHING'S DEFINITELY NOT RIGHT.
I'M ON IT.
TAP! TAP! TAP!
THE SPACE CENTER'S COMPUTER SYSTEM IS BEING JAMMED, KIM. I THINK SOMETHING'S UP.
C'MON, RON. WE'VE GOT TO GET A LOOK INSIDE.

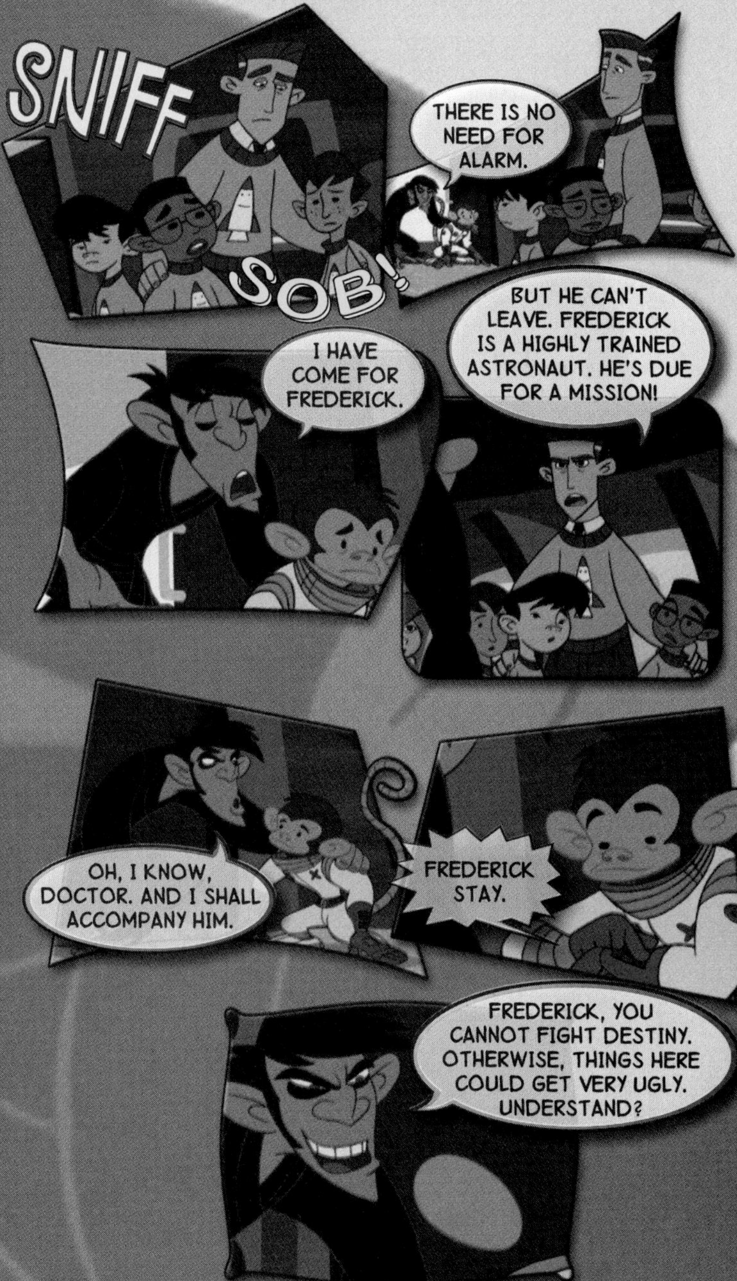
SNIFF
SOB!
THERE IS NO NEED FOR ALARM.
I HAVE COME FOR FREDERICK.
BUT HE CAN'T LEAVE. FREDERICK IS A HIGHLY TRAINED ASTRONAUT. HE'S DUE FOR A MISSION!
OH, I KNOW, DOCTOR. AND I SHALL ACCOMPANY HIM.
FREDERICK STAY.
FREDERICK, YOU CANNOT FIGHT DESTINY. OTHERWISE, THINGS HERE COULD GET VERY UGLY. UNDERSTAND?

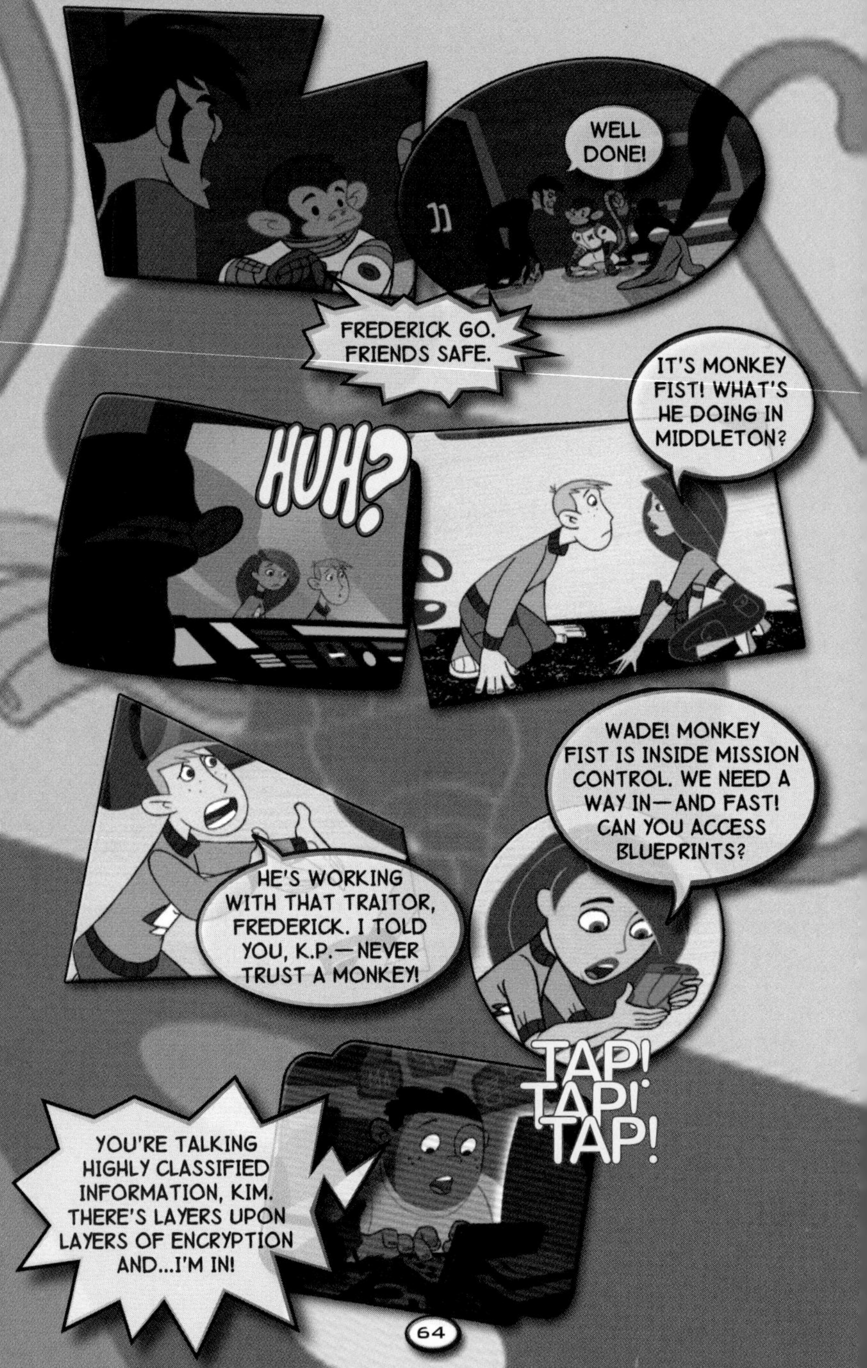
WELL DONE!
FREDERICK GO. FRIENDS SAFE.
HUH?
IT'S MONKEY FIST! WHAT'S HE DOING IN MIDDLETON?
HE'S WORKING WITH THAT TRAITOR, FREDERICK. I TOLD YOU, K.P.—NEVER TRUST A MONKEY!
WADE! MONKEY FIST IS INSIDE MISSION CONTROL. WE NEED A WAY IN—AND FAST! CAN YOU ACCESS BLUEPRINTS?
TAP! TAP! TAP!
YOU'RE TALKING HIGHLY CLASSIFIED INFORMATION, KIM. THERE'S LAYERS UPON LAYERS OF ENCRYPTION AND...I'M IN!

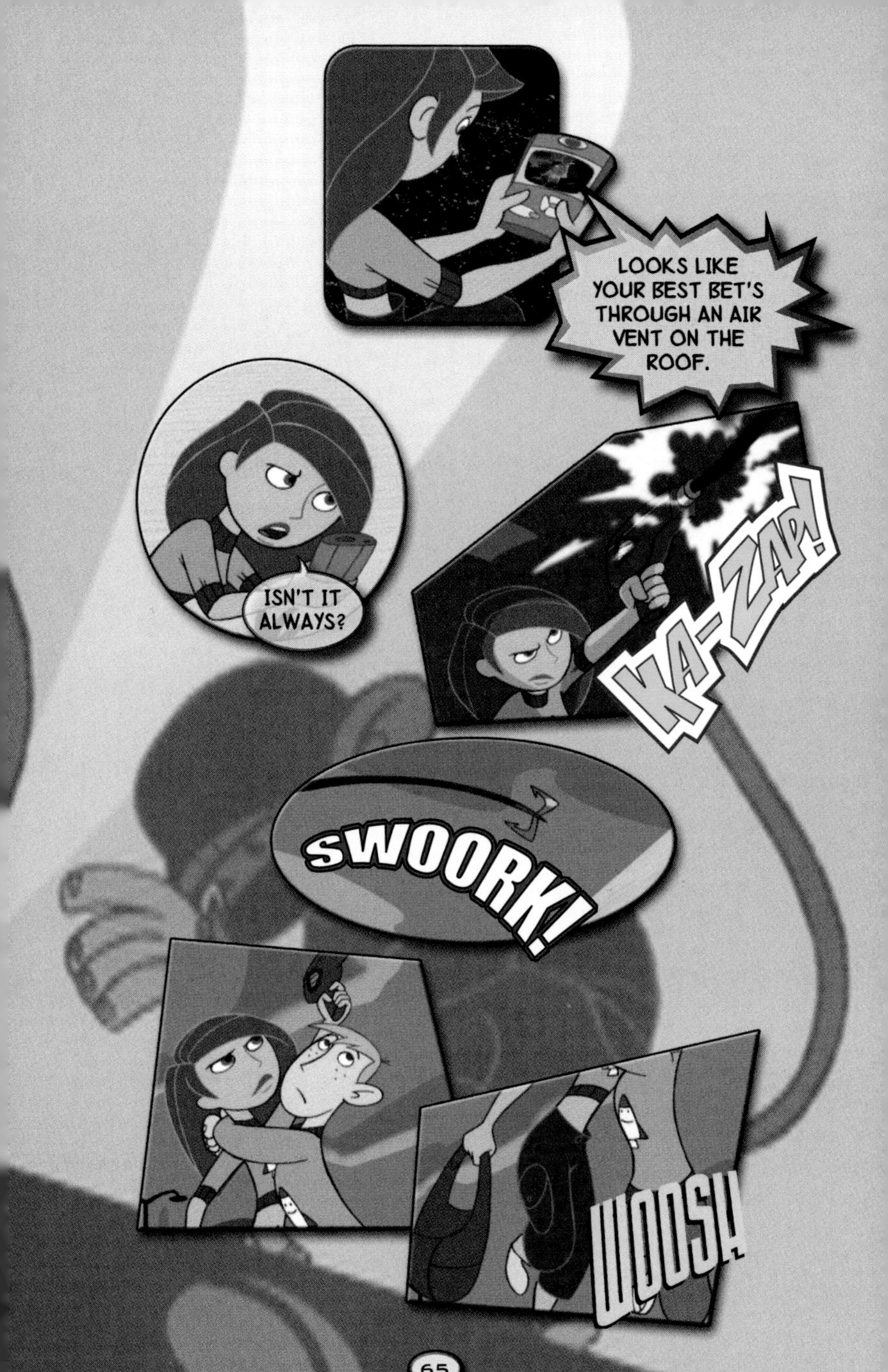
LOOKS LIKE YOUR BEST BET'S THROUGH AN AIR VENT ON THE ROOF.
ISN'T IT ALWAYS?
KA-ZAP!
SWOORK!
WOOSH

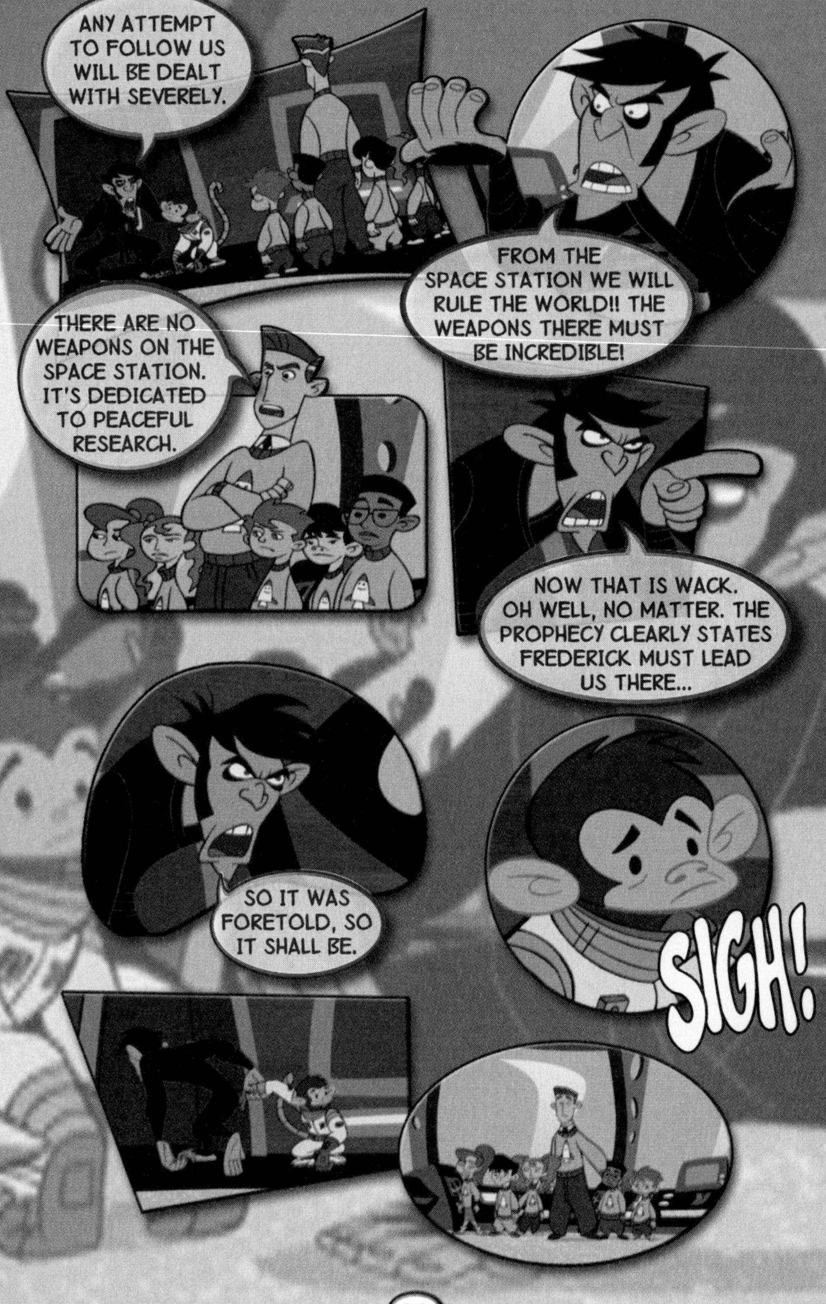
ANY ATTEMPT TO FOLLOW US WILL BE DEALT WITH SEVERELY.
FROM THE SPACE STATION WE WILL RULE THE WORLD!! THE WEAPONS THERE MUST BE INCREDIBLE!
THERE ARE NO WEAPONS ON THE SPACE STATION. IT'S DEDICATED TO PEACEFUL RESEARCH.
NOW THAT IS WACK. OH WELL, NO MATTER. THE PROPHECY CLEARLY STATES FREDERICK MUST LEAD US THERE...
SO IT WAS FORETOLD, SO IT SHALL BE.
SIGH!

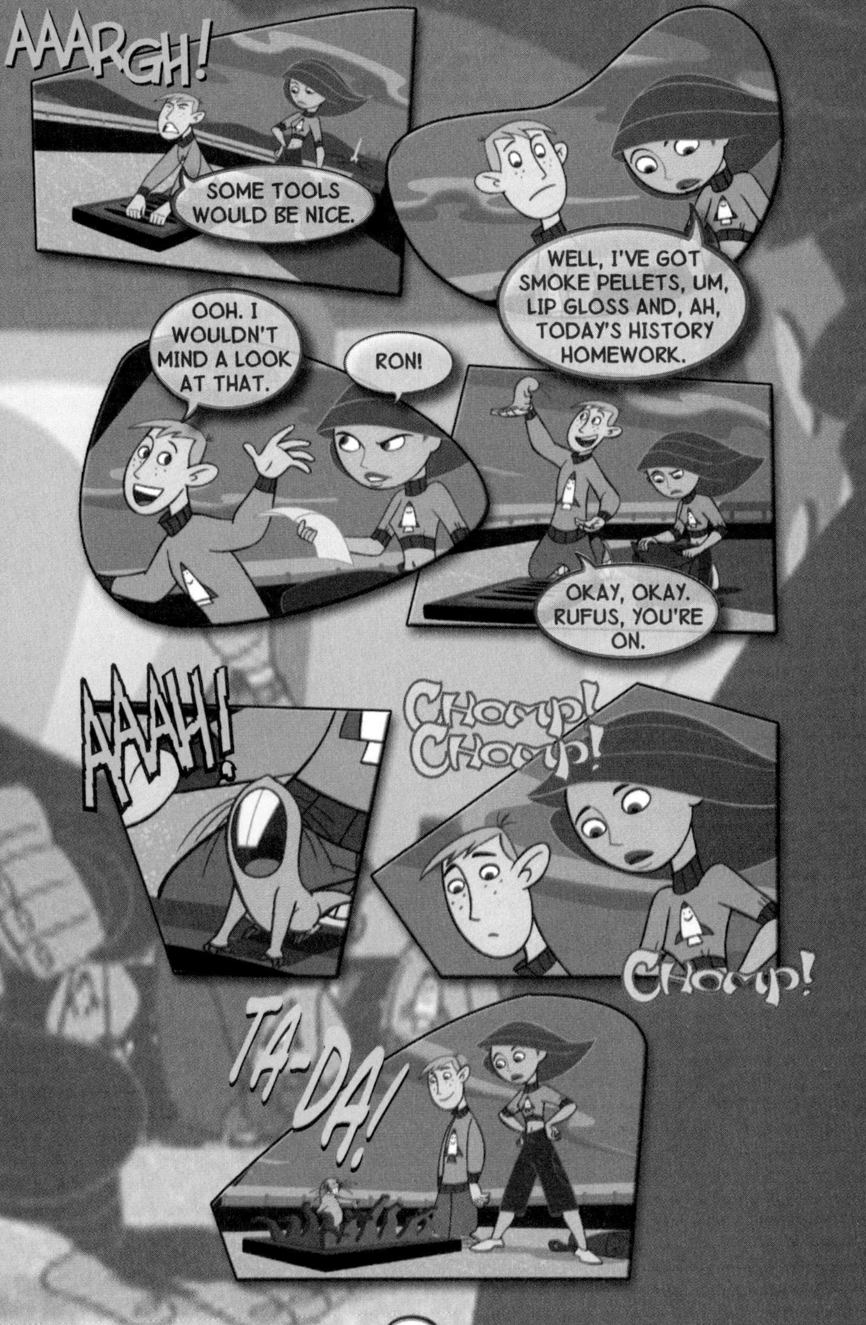
AAARGH!
SOME TOOLS WOULD BE NICE.
WELL, I'VE GOT SMOKE PELLETS, UM, LIP GLOSS AND, AH, TODAY'S HISTORY HOMEWORK.
OOH. I WOULDN'T MIND A LOOK AT THAT.
RON!
OKAY, OKAY. RUFUS, YOU'RE ON.
AAAH!
CHOMP! CHOMP!
CHOMP!
TA-DA!

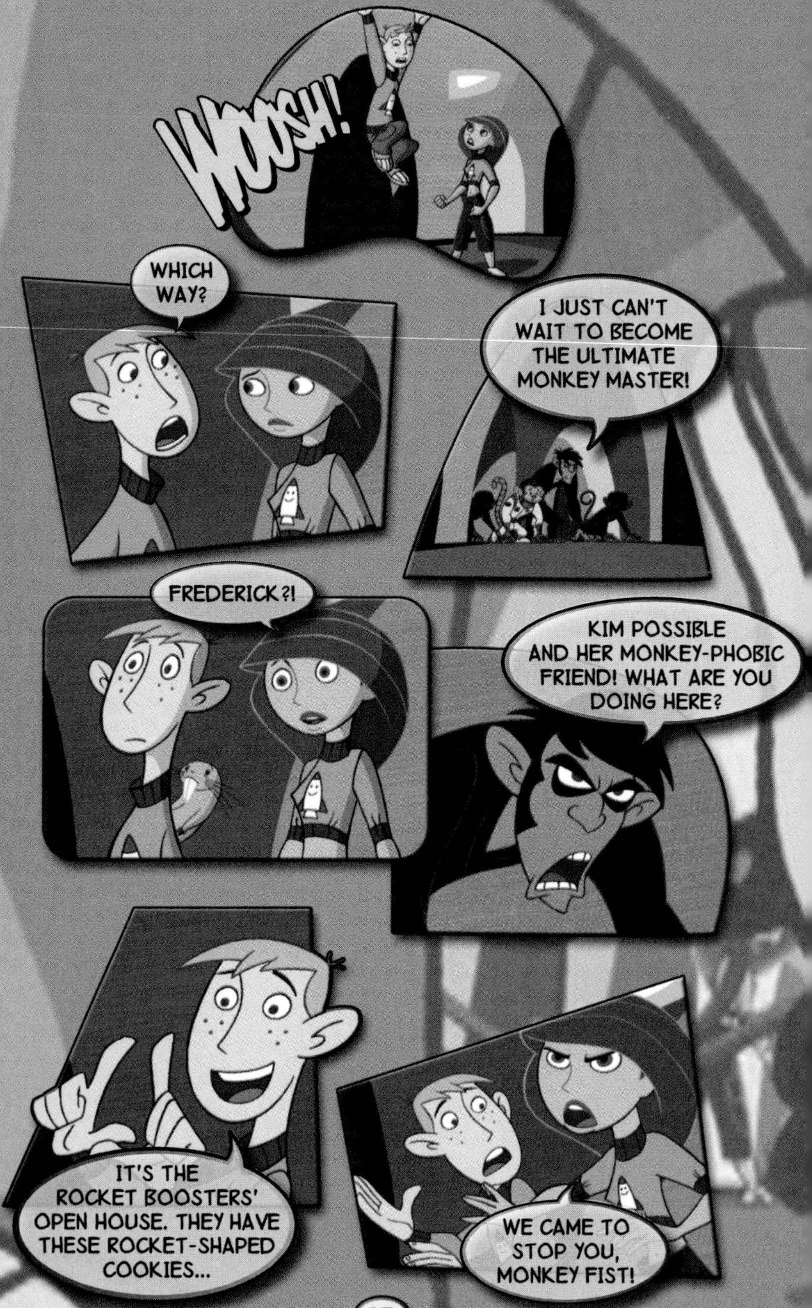
WHOOSH!
WHICH WAY?
I JUST CAN'T WAIT TO BECOME THE ULTIMATE MONKEY MASTER!
FREDERICK?!
KIM POSSIBLE AND HER MONKEY-PHOBIC FRIEND! WHAT ARE YOU DOING HERE?
IT'S THE ROCKET BOOSTERS' OPEN HOUSE. THEY HAVE THESE ROCKET-SHAPED COOKIES...
WE CAME TO STOP YOU, MONKEY FIST!

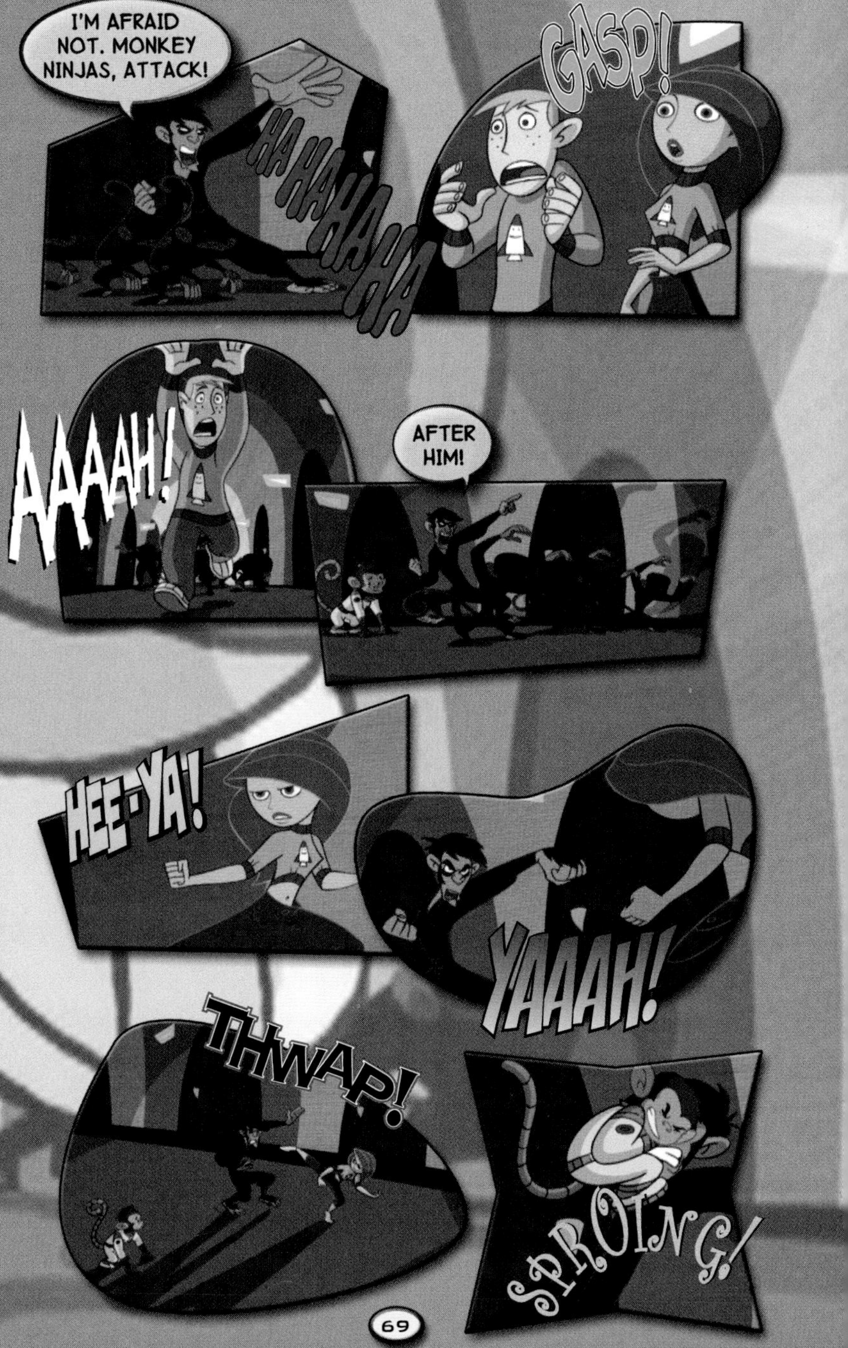
I'M AFRAID NOT. MONKEY NINJAS, ATTACK!
HA HA HA HA HA HA
GASP!
AAAAH!
AFTER HIM!
HEE-YA!
YAAAH!
THWAP!
SPROING!

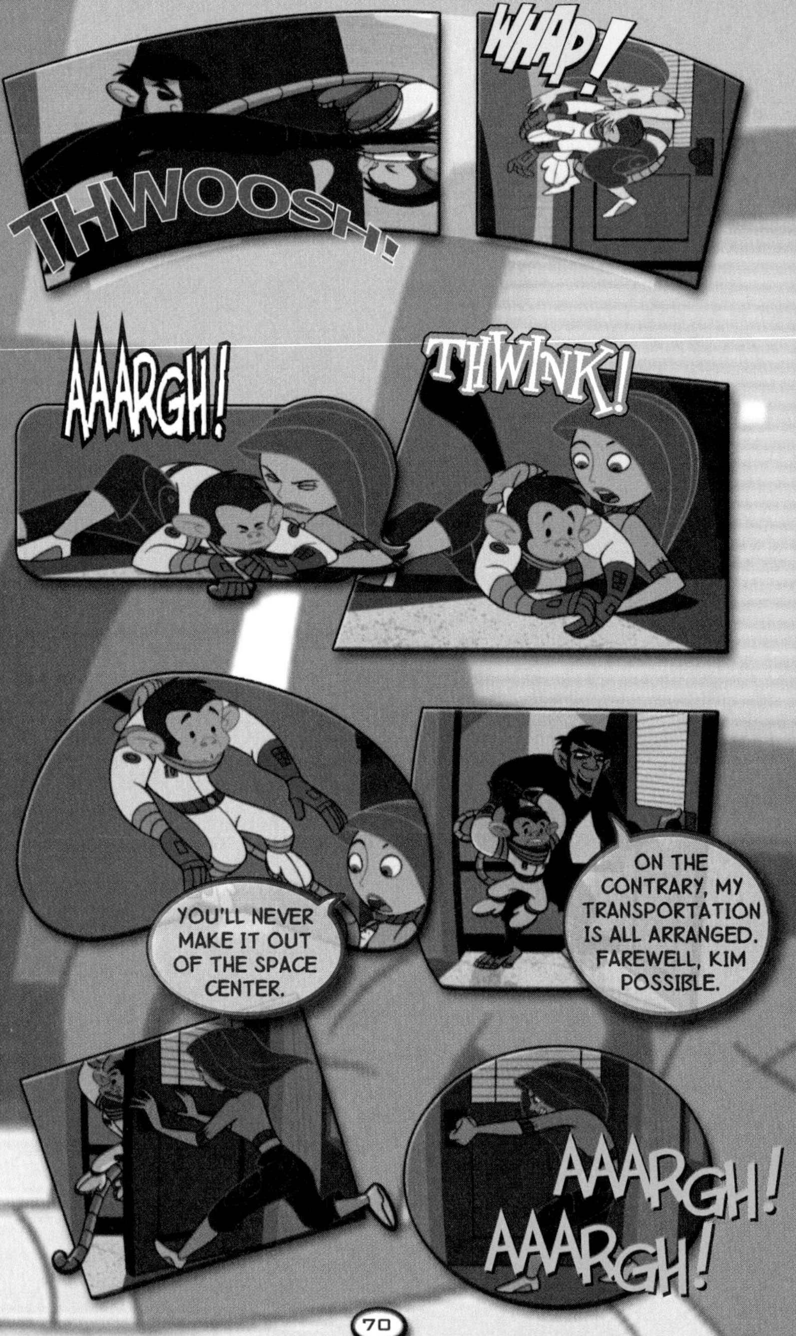
THWOOSH!
WHAP!
AAARGH!
THWINK!
YOU'LL NEVER MAKE IT OUT OF THE SPACE CENTER.
ON THE CONTRARY, MY TRANSPORTATION IS ALL ARRANGED. FAREWELL, KIM POSSIBLE.
AAARGH!
AAARGH!

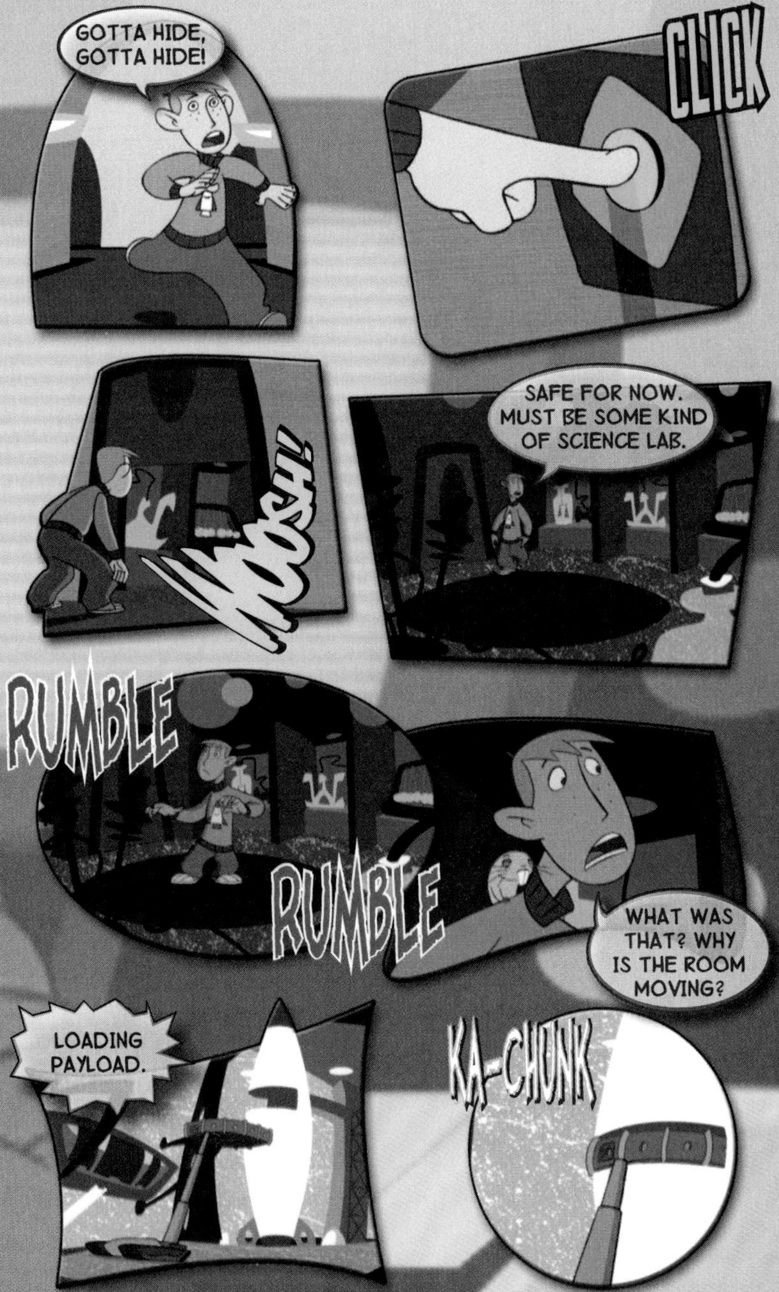
GOTTA HIDE, GOTTA HIDE!
CLICK
WOOSH!
SAFE FOR NOW. MUST BE SOME KIND OF SCIENCE LAB.
RUMBLE
RUMBLE
WHAT WAS THAT? WHY IS THE ROOM MOVING?
LOADING PAYLOAD.
KA-CHUNK

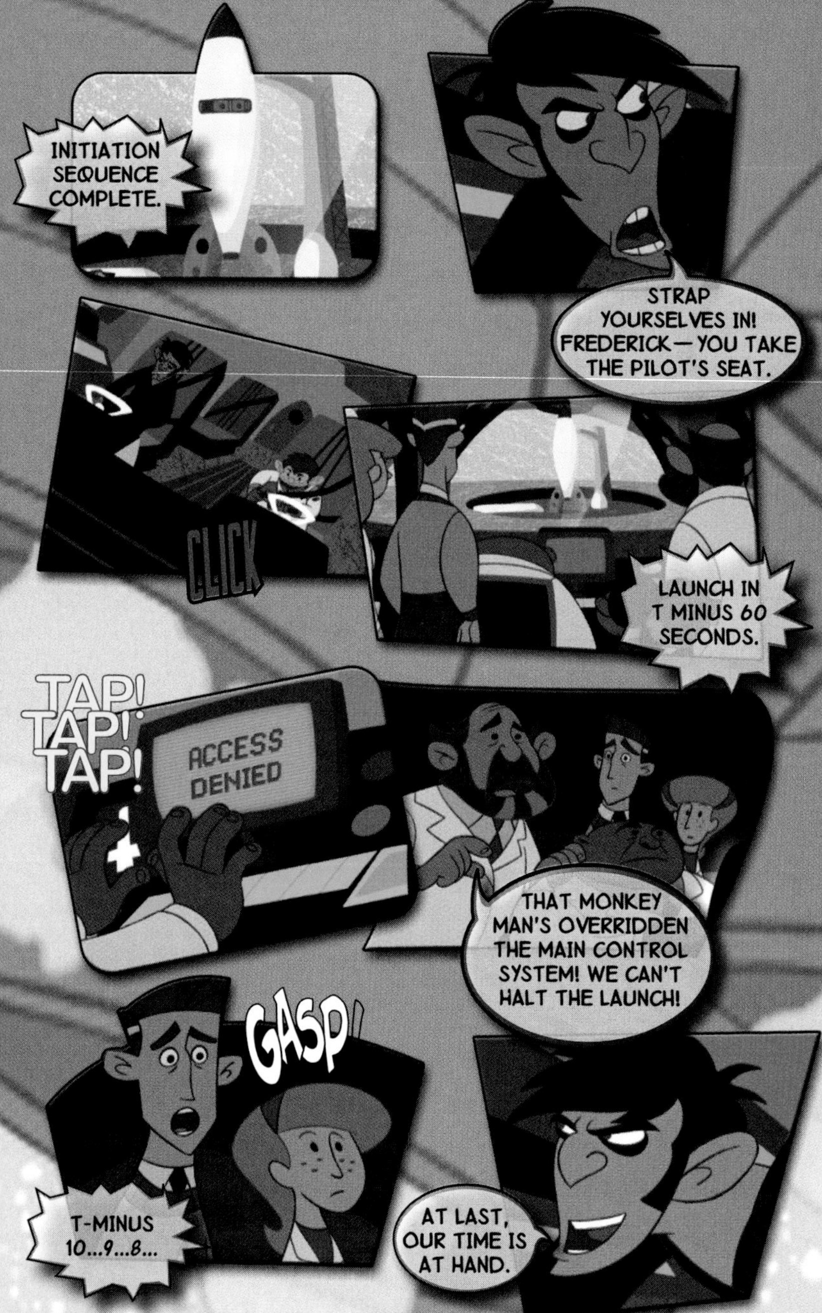
INITIATION SEQUENCE COMPLETE.
STRAP YOURSELVES IN! FREDERICK—YOU TAKE THE PILOT'S SEAT.
CLICK
LAUNCH IN T MINUS 60 SECONDS.
TAP! TAP! TAP!
ACCESS DENIED
THAT MONKEY MAN'S OVERRIDDEN THE MAIN CONTROL SYSTEM! WE CAN'T HALT THE LAUNCH!
GASP!
T-MINUS 10...9...8...
AT LAST, OUR TIME IS AT HAND.

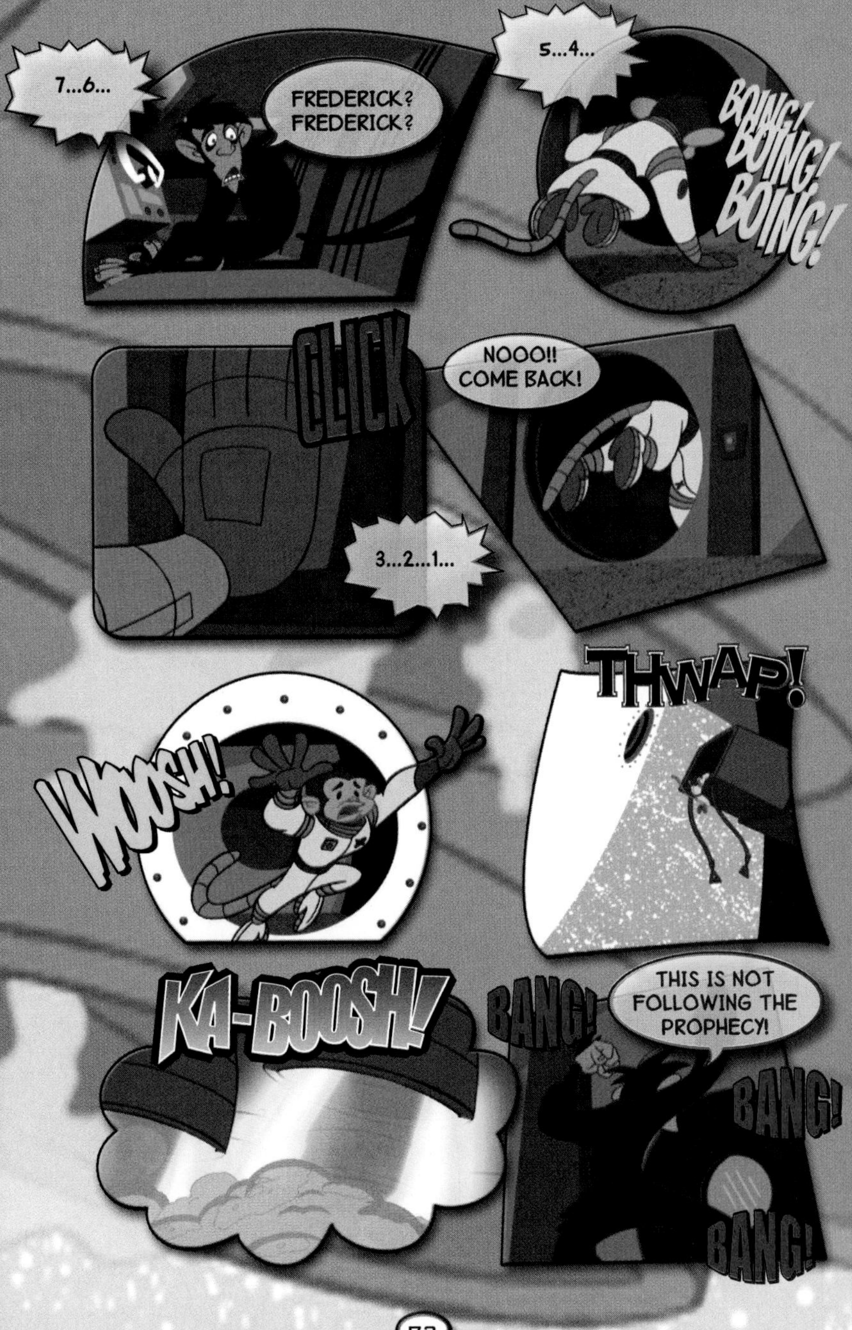
7...6...
FREDERICK? FREDERICK?
5...4...
BOING! BOING! BOING!
CLICK
NOOO!! COME BACK!
3...2...1...
WOOSH!
THWAP!
KA-BOOSH!
BANG!
THIS IS NOT FOLLOWING THE PROPHECY!
BANG!
BANG!

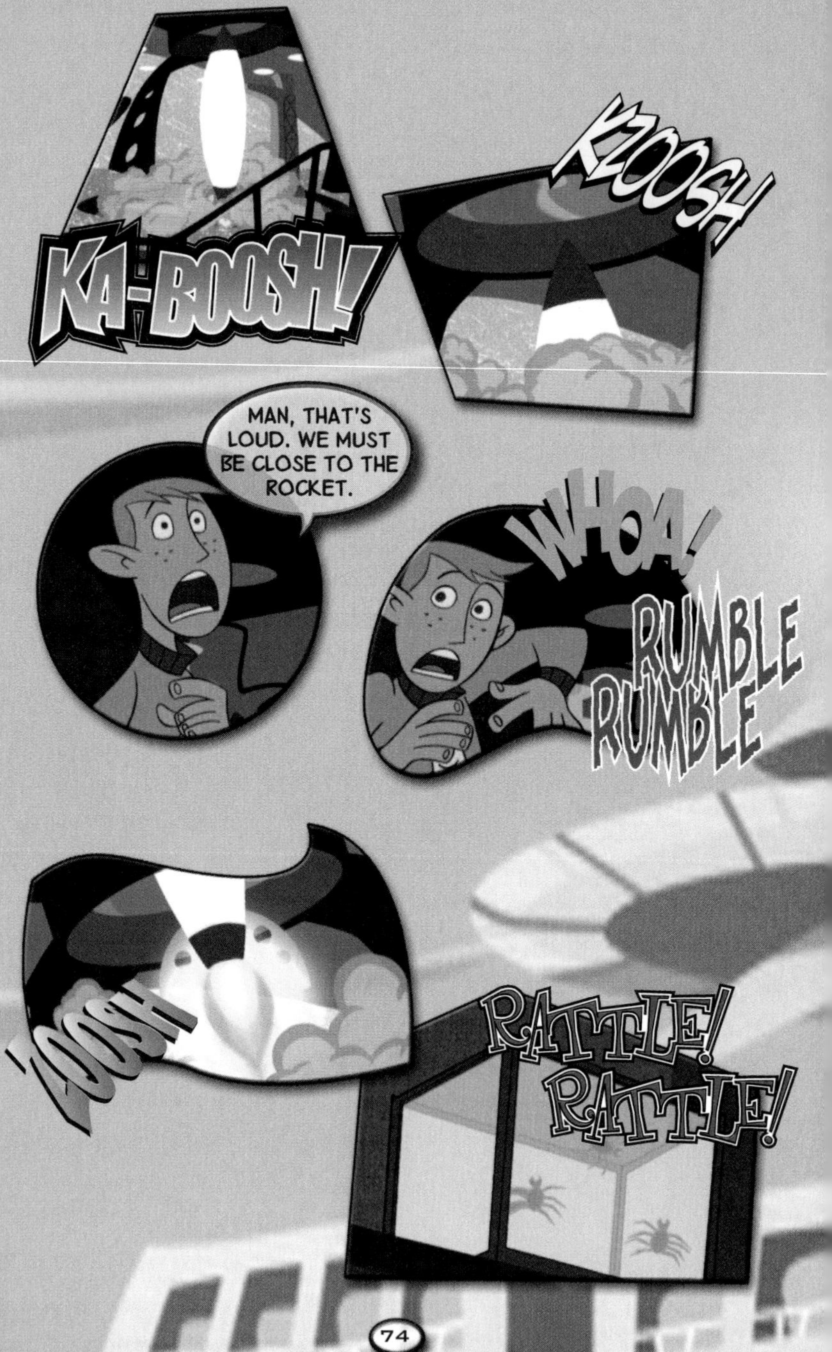
KA-BOOSH!
KZOOSH
MAN, THAT'S LOUD. WE MUST BE CLOSE TO THE ROCKET.
WHOA!
RUMBLE RUMBLE
OOSH
RATTLE! RATTLE!

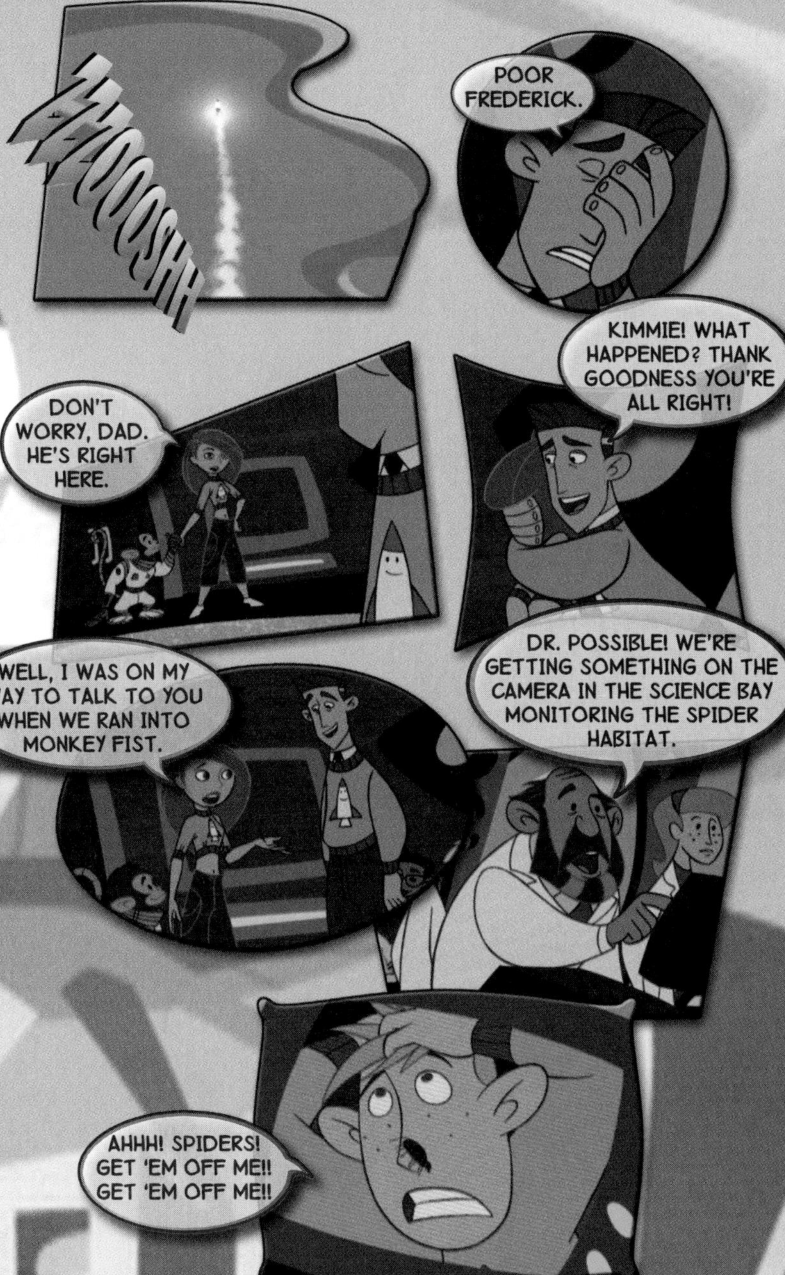
ZHOOSH
POOR FREDERICK.
DON'T WORRY, DAD. HE'S RIGHT HERE.
KIMMIE! WHAT HAPPENED? THANK GOODNESS YOU'RE ALL RIGHT!
WELL, I WAS ON MY WAY TO TALK TO YOU WHEN WE RAN INTO MONKEY FIST.
DR. POSSIBLE! WE'RE GETTING SOMETHING ON THE CAMERA IN THE SCIENCE BAY MONITORING THE SPIDER HABITAT.
AHHH! SPIDERS! GET 'EM OFF ME!! GET 'EM OFF ME!!

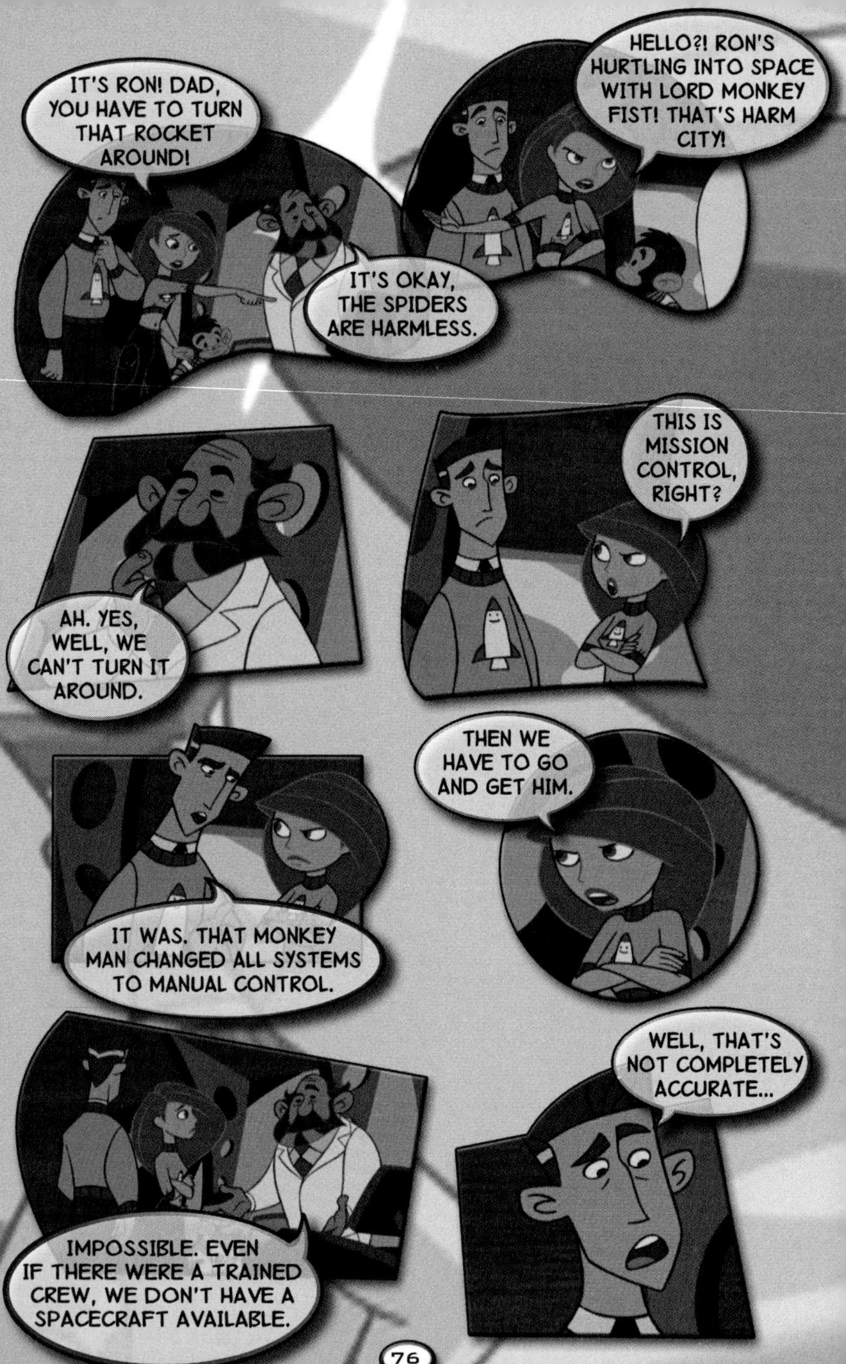

IT'S RON! DAD, YOU HAVE TO TURN THAT ROCKET AROUND!
IT'S OKAY, THE SPIDERS ARE HARMLESS.
HELLO?! RON'S HURTLING INTO SPACE WITH LORD MONKEY FIST! THAT'S HARM CITY!
AH. YES, WELL, WE CAN'T TURN IT AROUND.
THIS IS MISSION CONTROL, RIGHT?
IT WAS. THAT MONKEY MAN CHANGED ALL SYSTEMS TO MANUAL CONTROL.
THEN WE HAVE TO GO AND GET HIM.
IMPOSSIBLE. EVEN IF THERE WERE A TRAINED CREW, WE DON'T HAVE A SPACECRAFT AVAILABLE.
WELL, THAT'S NOT COMPLETELY ACCURATE...

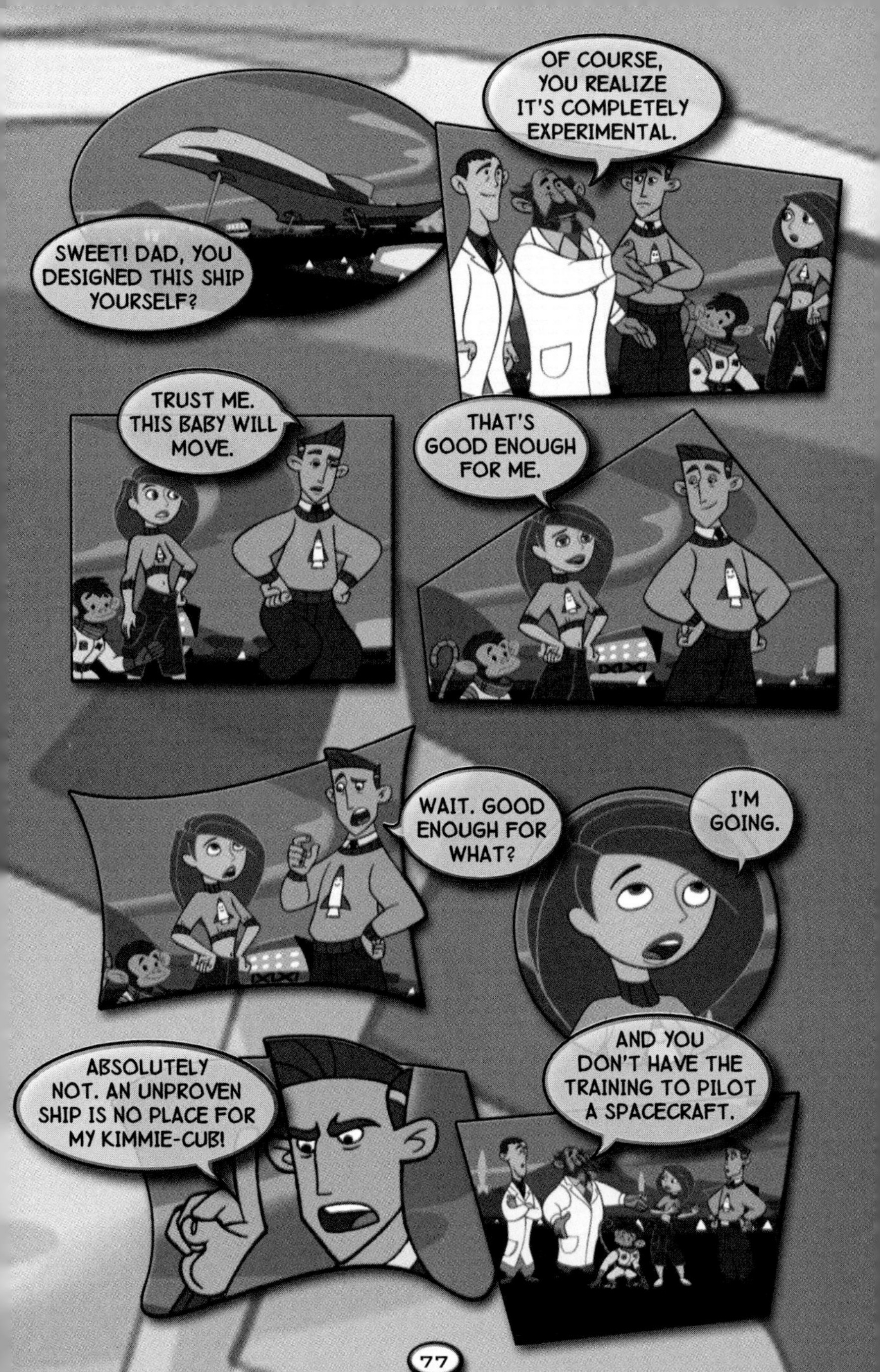

SWEET! DAD, YOU DESIGNED THIS SHIP YOURSELF?
OF COURSE, YOU REALIZE IT'S COMPLETELY EXPERIMENTAL.
TRUST ME. THIS BABY WILL MOVE.
THAT'S GOOD ENOUGH FOR ME.
WAIT. GOOD ENOUGH FOR WHAT?
I'M GOING.
ABSOLUTELY NOT. AN UNPROVEN SHIP IS NO PLACE FOR MY KIMMIE-CUB!
AND YOU DON'T HAVE THE TRAINING TO PILOT A SPACECRAFT.

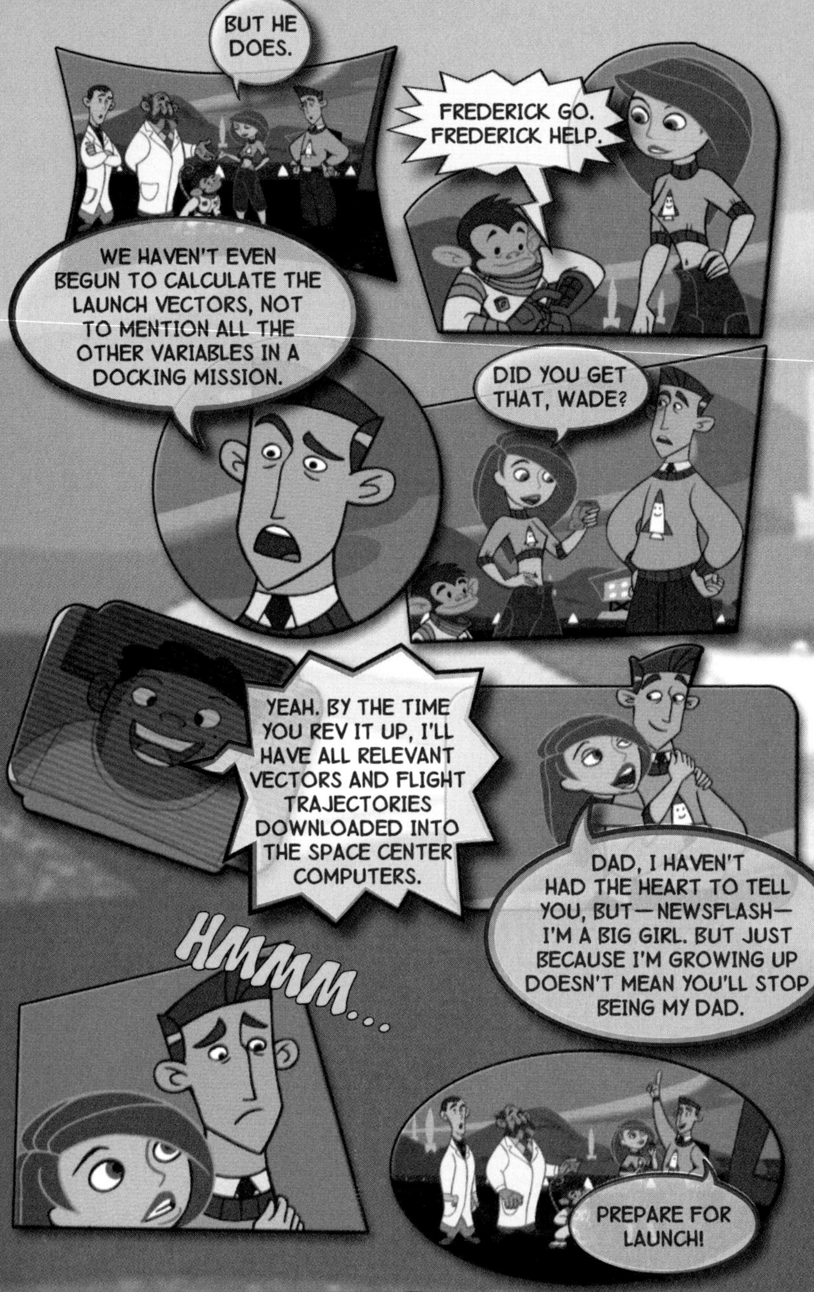
BUT HE DOES.
FREDERICK GO. FREDERICK HELP.
WE HAVEN'T EVEN BEGUN TO CALCULATE THE LAUNCH VECTORS, NOT TO MENTION ALL THE OTHER VARIABLES IN A DOCKING MISSION.
DID YOU GET THAT, WADE?
YEAH. BY THE TIME YOU REV IT UP, I'LL HAVE ALL RELEVANT VECTORS AND FLIGHT TRAJECTORIES DOWNLOADED INTO THE SPACE CENTER COMPUTERS.
DAD, I HAVEN'T HAD THE HEART TO TELL YOU, BUT—NEWSFLASH—I'M A BIG GIRL. BUT JUST BECAUSE I'M GROWING UP DOESN'T MEAN YOU'LL STOP BEING MY DAD.
HMMM...
PREPARE FOR LAUNCH!

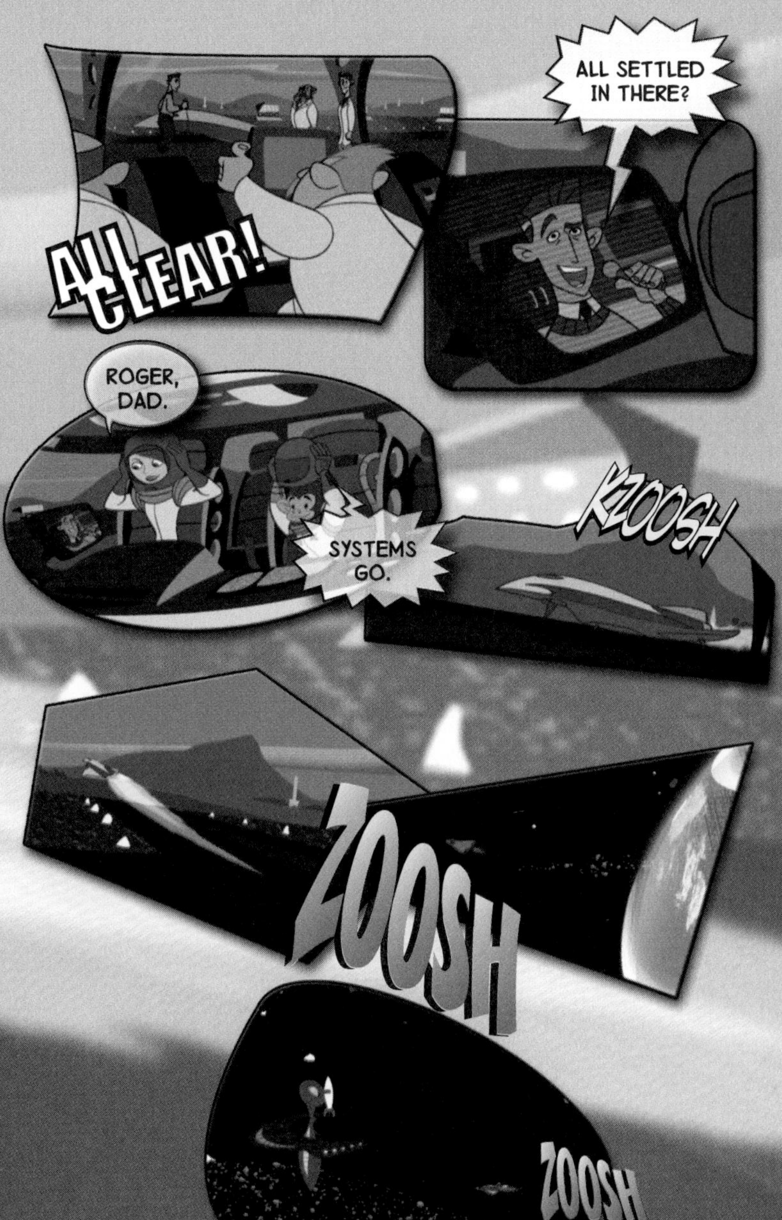
ALL CLEAR!
ALL SETTLED IN THERE?
ROGER, DAD.
SYSTEMS GO.
KZOOSH
ZOOSH
ZOOSH

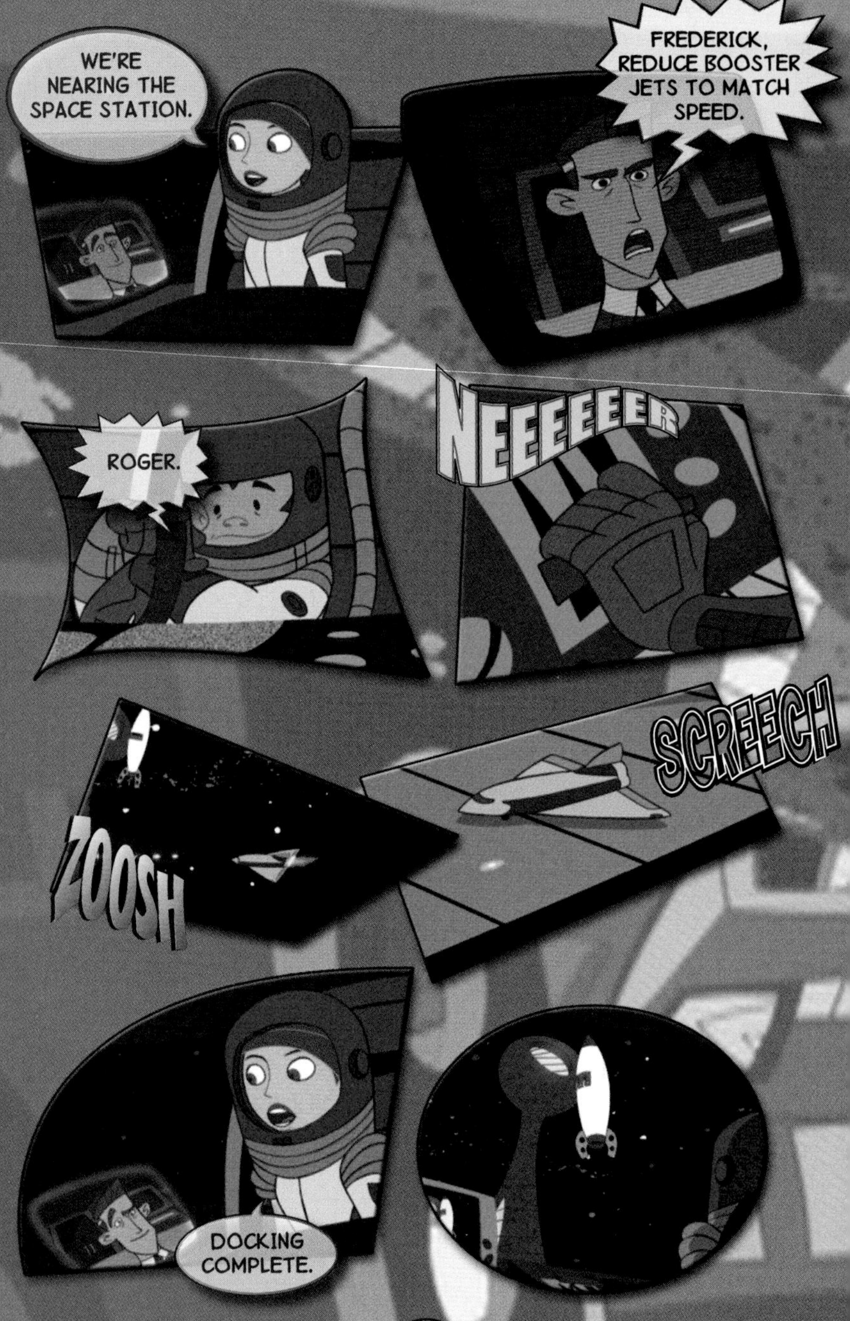

WE'RE NEARING THE SPACE STATION.
FREDERICK, REDUCE BOOSTER JETS TO MATCH SPEED.
ROGER.
NEEEEEER
ZOOSH
SCREECH
DOCKING COMPLETE.

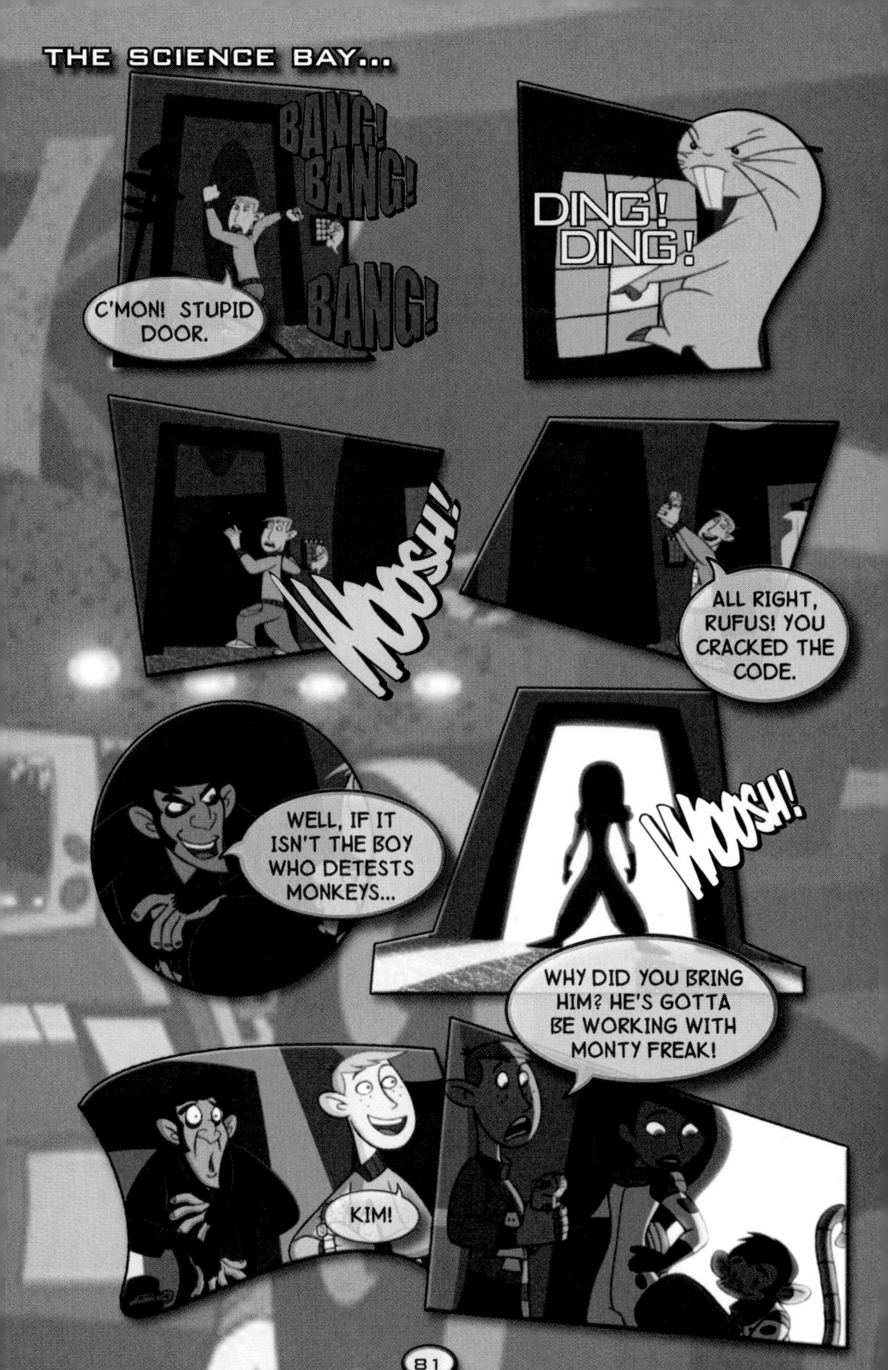
THE SCIENCE BAY...
BANG! BANG!
BANG!
C'MON! STUPID DOOR.
DING! DING!
WOOSH!
ALL RIGHT, RUFUS! YOU CRACKED THE CODE.
WELL, IF IT ISN'T THE BOY WHO DETESTS MONKEYS...
WOOSH!
WHY DID YOU BRING HIM? HE'S GOTTA BE WORKING WITH MONTY FREAK!
KIM!

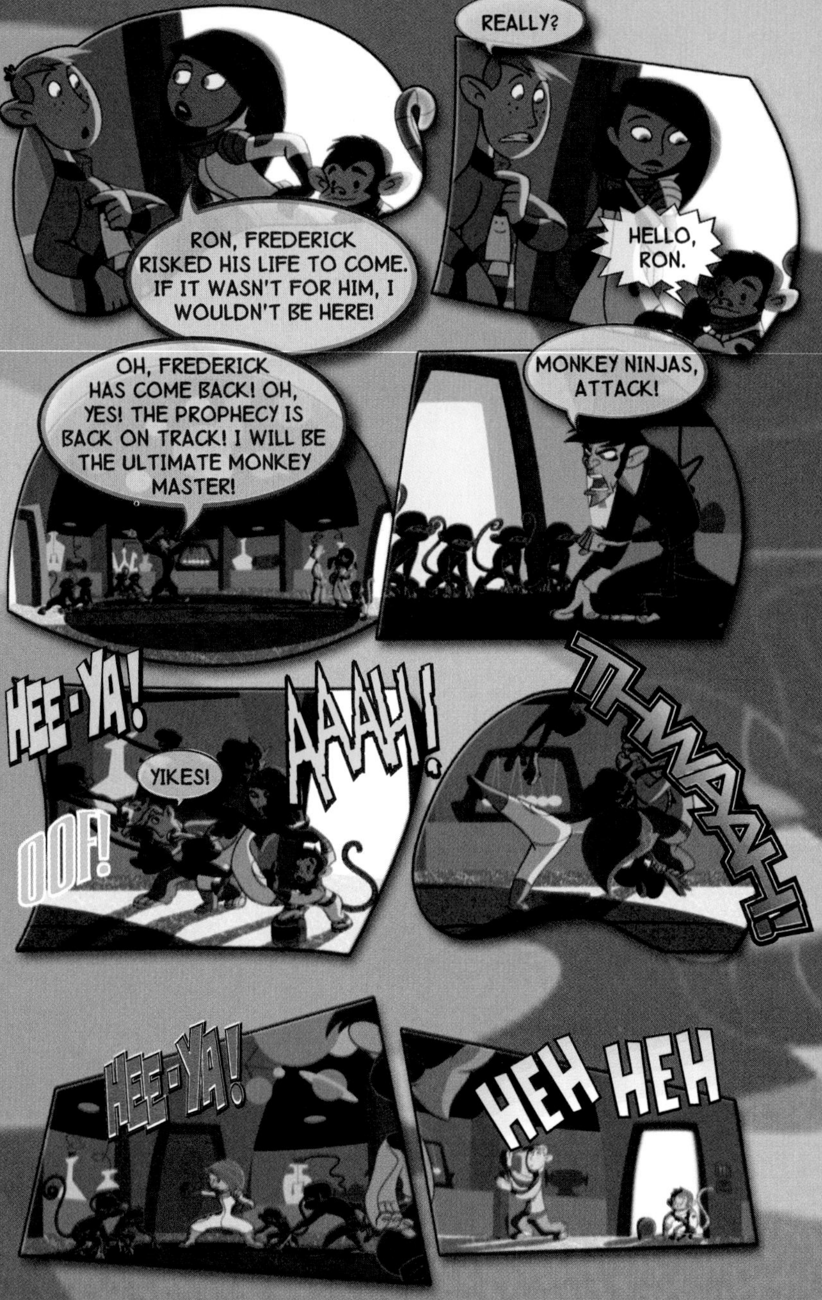
RON, FREDERICK RISKED HIS LIFE TO COME. IF IT WASN'T FOR HIM, I WOULDN'T BE HERE!
REALLY?
HELLO, RON.
OH, FREDERICK HAS COME BACK! OH, YES! THE PROPHECY IS BACK ON TRACK! I WILL BE THE ULTIMATE MONKEY MASTER!
MONKEY NINJAS, ATTACK!
HEE-YA!
YIKES!
OOF!
AAAH!
THWAAAH!
HEE-YA!
HEH HEH

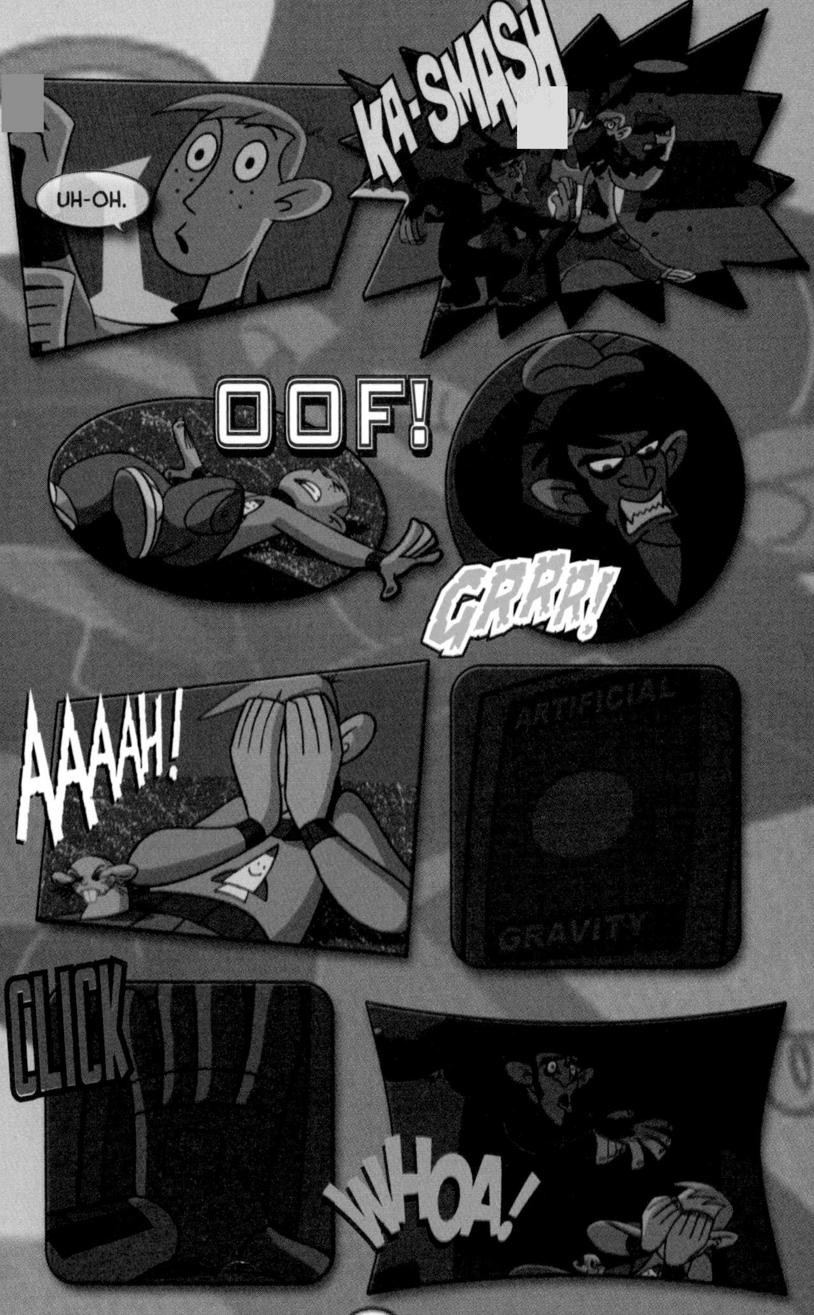
UH-OH.
KA-SMASH
OOF!
GRRR!
AAAAH!
ARTIFICIAL
GRAVITY
CLICK
WHOA!

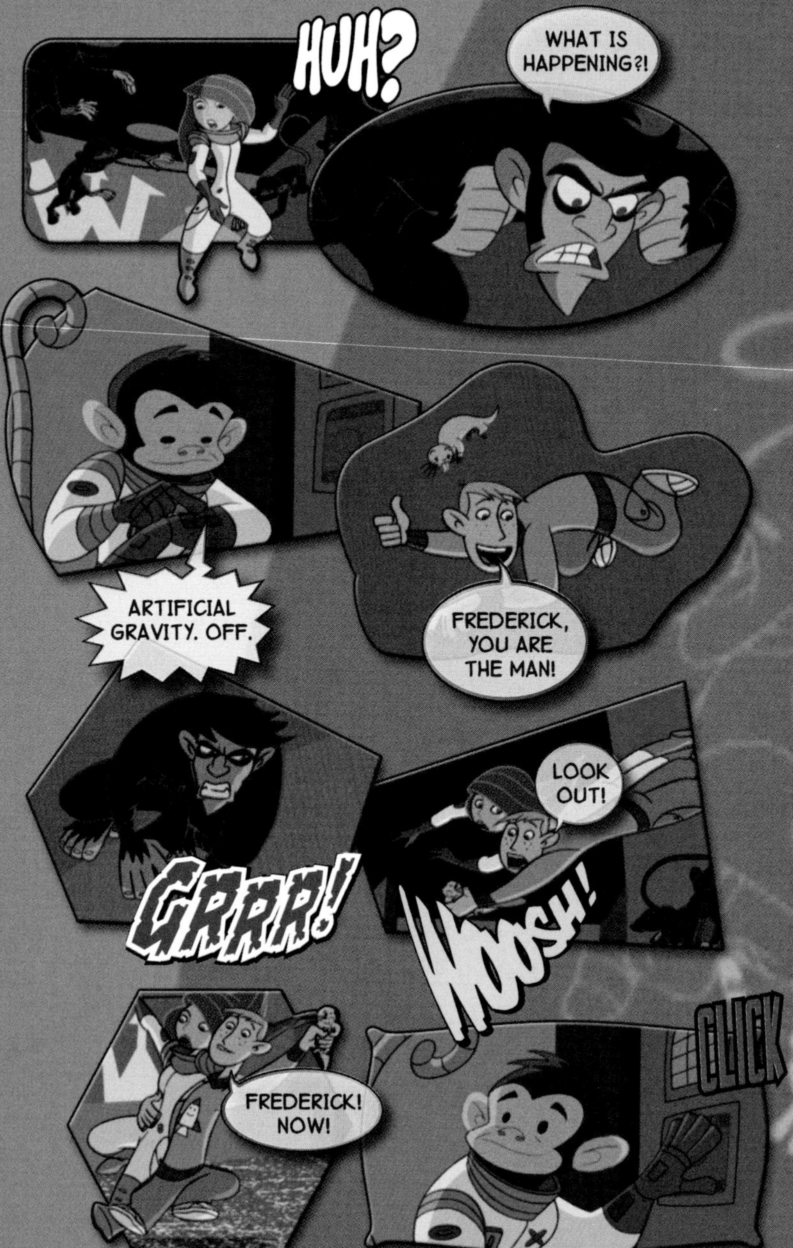
HUH?
WHAT IS HAPPENING?!
ARTIFICIAL GRAVITY. OFF.
FREDERICK, YOU ARE THE MAN!
GRRR!
LOOK OUT!
WOOSH!
FREDERICK! NOW!
CLICK

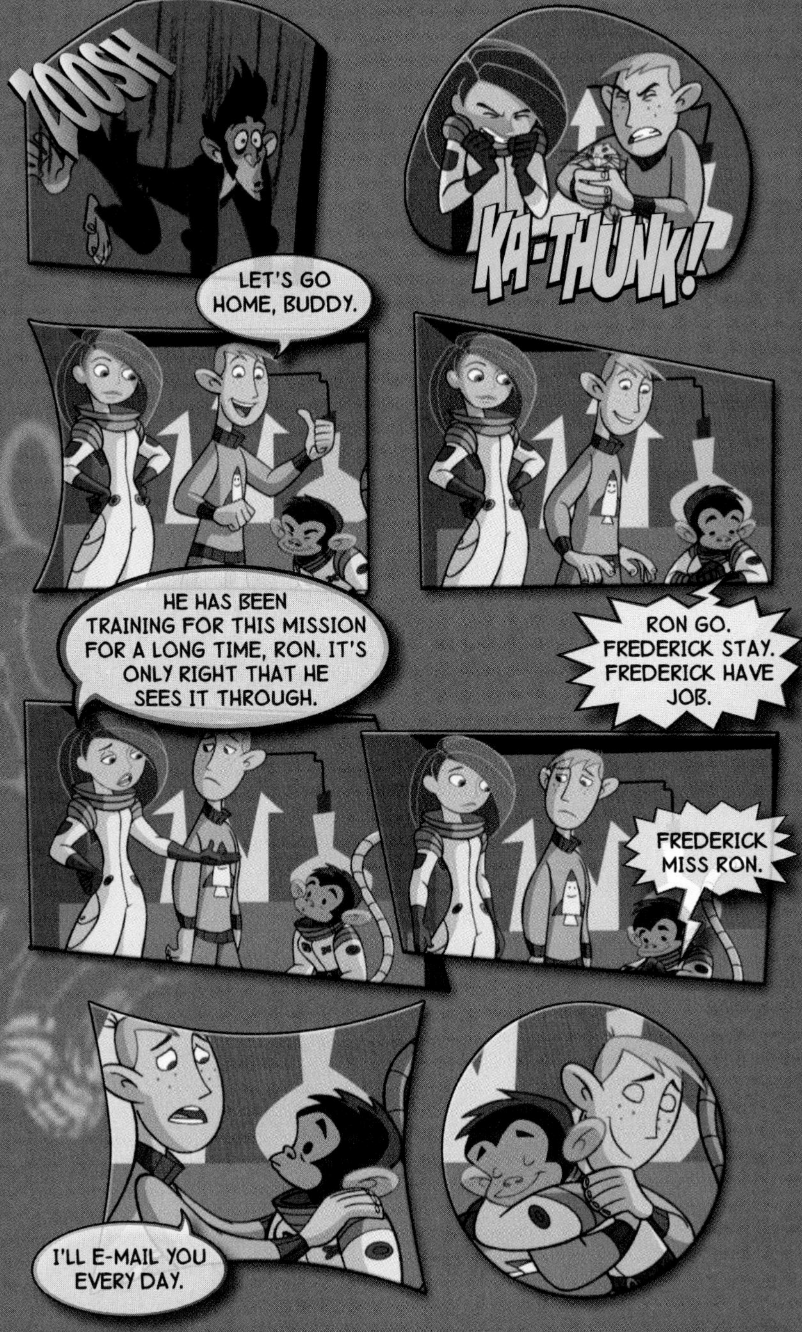
ZOOSH
KA-THUNK!
LET'S GO HOME, BUDDY.
HE HAS BEEN TRAINING FOR THIS MISSION FOR A LONG TIME, RON. IT'S ONLY RIGHT THAT HE SEES IT THROUGH.
RON GO. FREDERICK STAY. FREDERICK HAVE JOB.
FREDERICK MISS RON.
I'LL E-MAIL YOU EVERY DAY.

BACK ON EARTH...

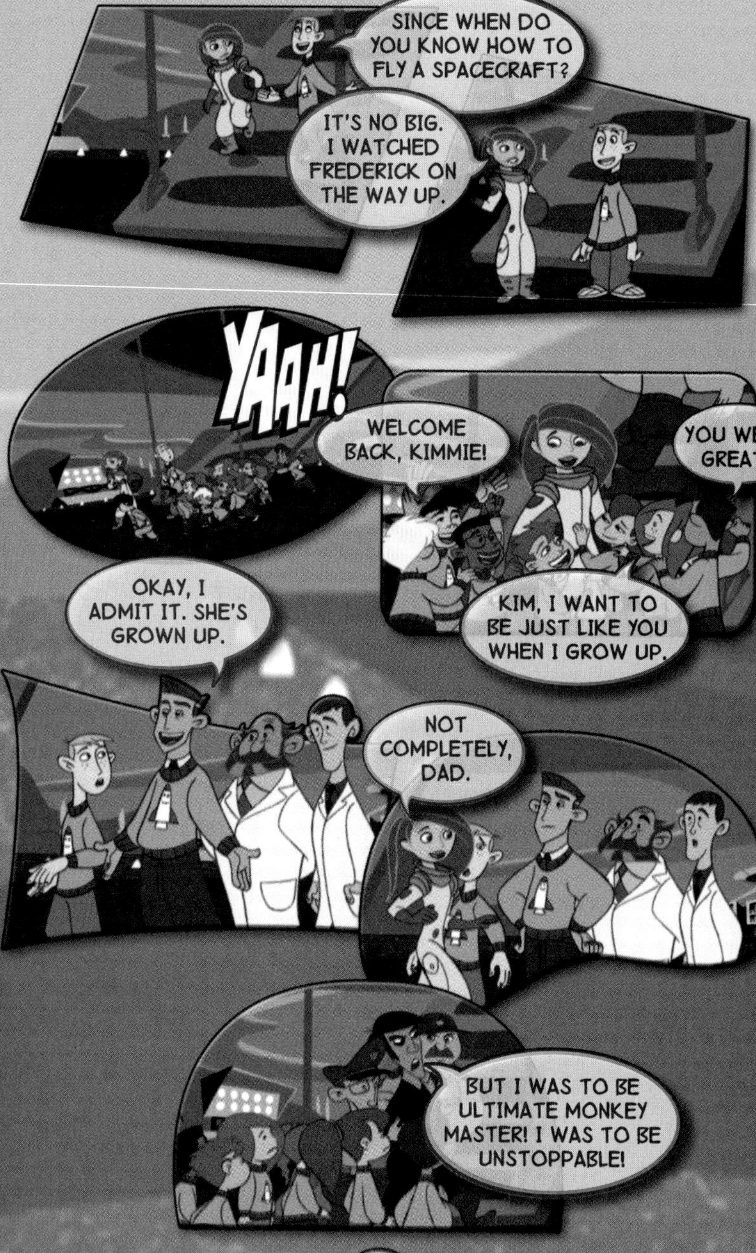
SINCE WHEN DO YOU KNOW HOW TO FLY A SPACECRAFT?
IT'S NO BIG. I WATCHED FREDERICK ON THE WAY UP.
YAAH!
WELCOME BACK, KIMMIE!
YOU WERE GREAT!
KIM, I WANT TO BE JUST LIKE YOU WHEN I GROW UP.
OKAY, I ADMIT IT. SHE'S GROWN UP.
NOT COMPLETELY, DAD.
BUT I WAS TO BE ULTIMATE MONKEY MASTER! I WAS TO BE UNSTOPPABLE!

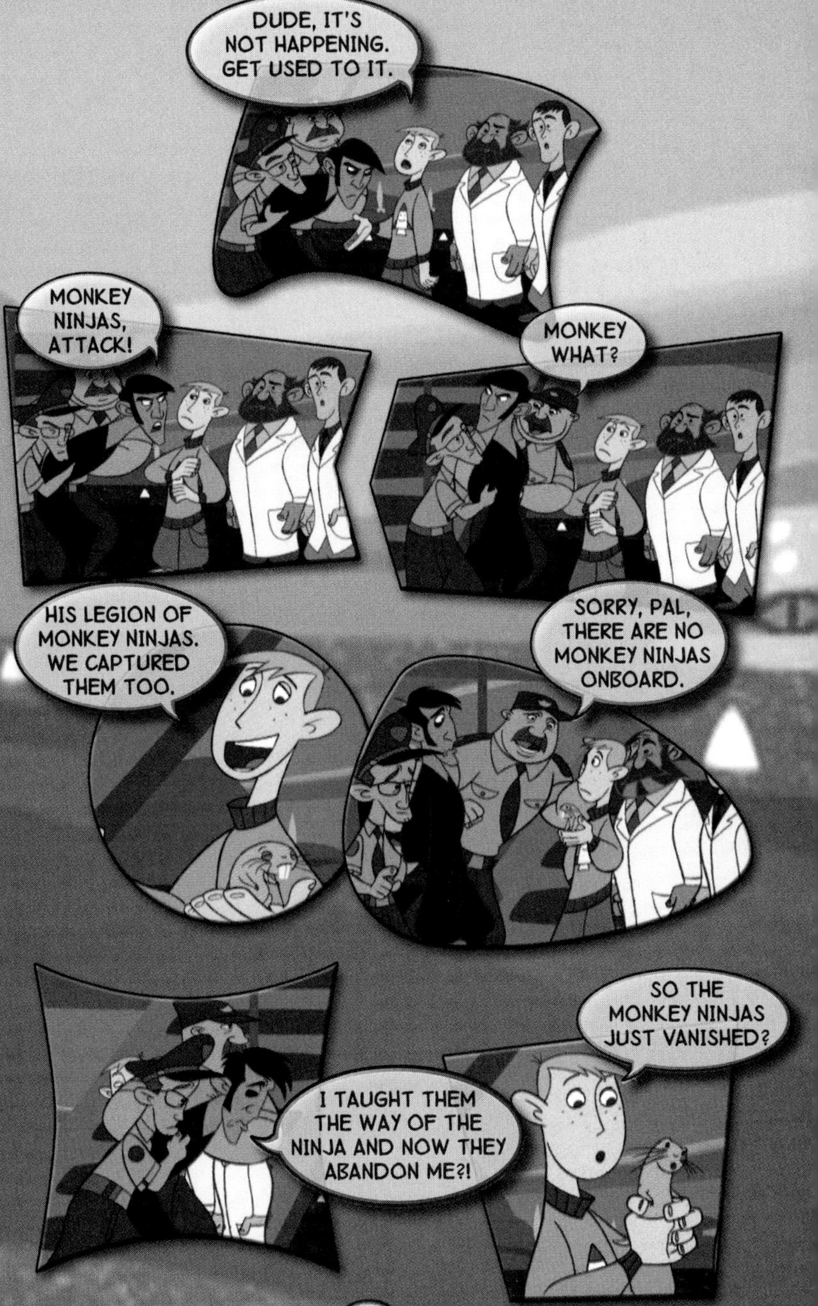
DUDE, IT'S NOT HAPPENING. GET USED TO IT.
MONKEY NINJAS, ATTACK!
MONKEY WHAT?
HIS LEGION OF MONKEY NINJAS. WE CAPTURED THEM TOO.
SORRY, PAL, THERE ARE NO MONKEY NINJAS ONBOARD.
I TAUGHT THEM THE WAY OF THE NINJA AND NOW THEY ABANDON ME?!
SO THE MONKEY NINJAS JUST VANISHED?

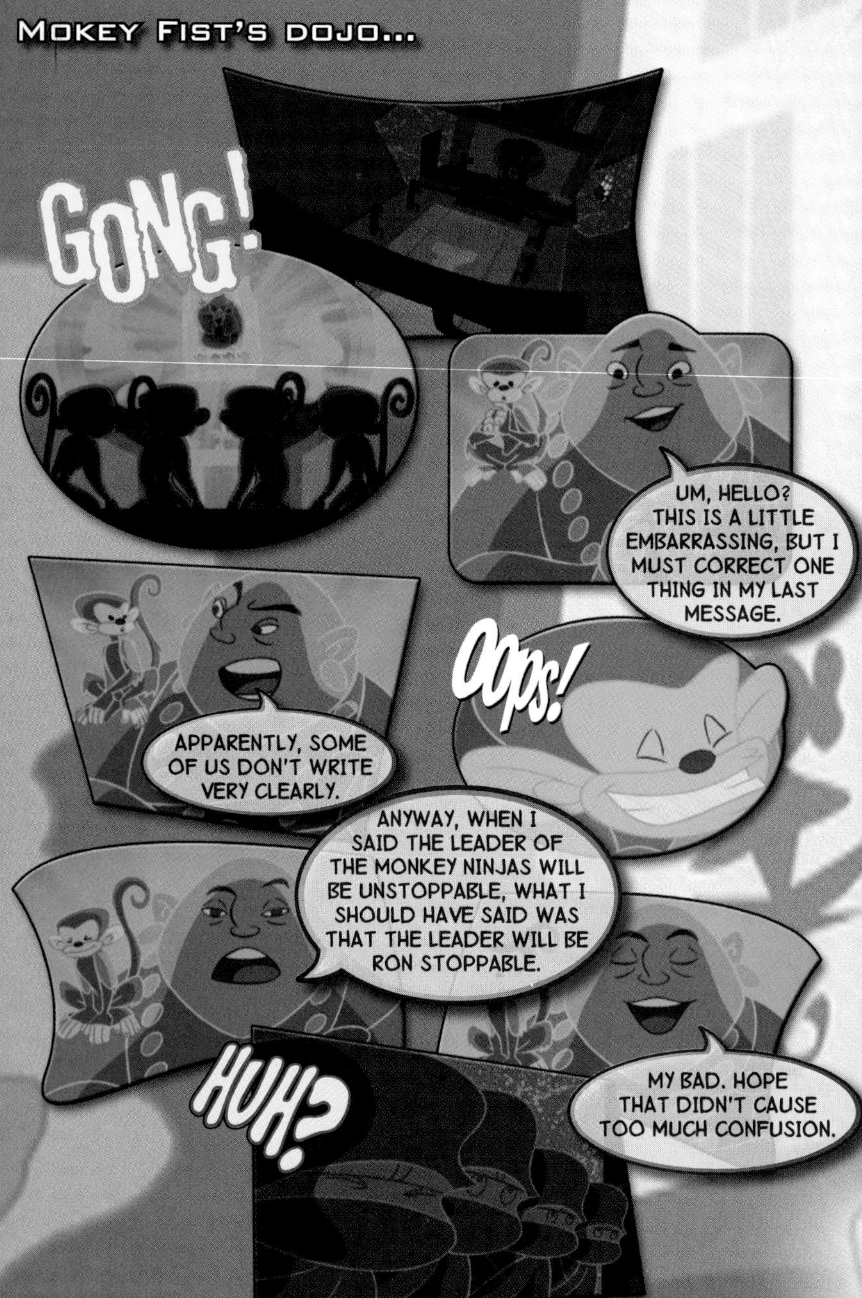
MOKEY FIST'S DOJO...
GONG!
UM, HELLO? THIS IS A LITTLE EMBARRASSING, BUT I MUST CORRECT ONE THING IN MY LAST MESSAGE.
APPARENTLY, SOME OF US DON'T WRITE VERY CLEARLY.
OOPS!
ANYWAY, WHEN I SAID THE LEADER OF THE MONKEY NINJAS WILL BE UNSTOPPABLE, WHAT I SHOULD HAVE SAID WAS THAT THE LEADER WILL BE RON STOPPABLE.
MY BAD. HOPE THAT DIDN'T CAUSE TOO MUCH CONFUSION.
HUH?

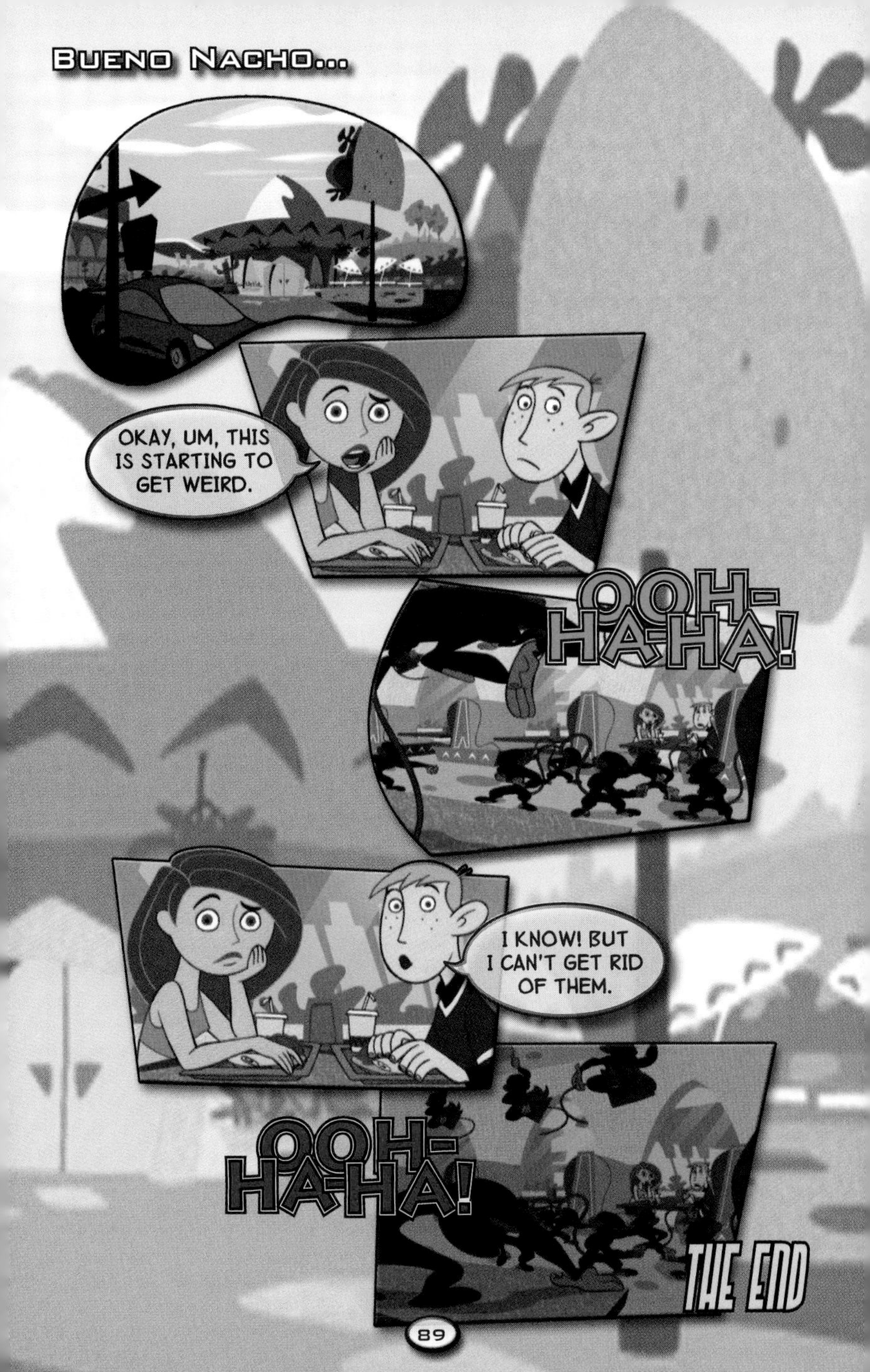
BUENO NACHO...
OKAY, UM, THIS IS STARTING TO GET WEIRD.
OOH-HA-HA!
I KNOW! BUT I CAN'T GET RID OF THEM.
OOH-HA-HA!
THE END

ALSO AVAILABLE FROM TOKYOPOP®

**For more
information visit
www.TOKYOPOP.com**

03.03.04Y

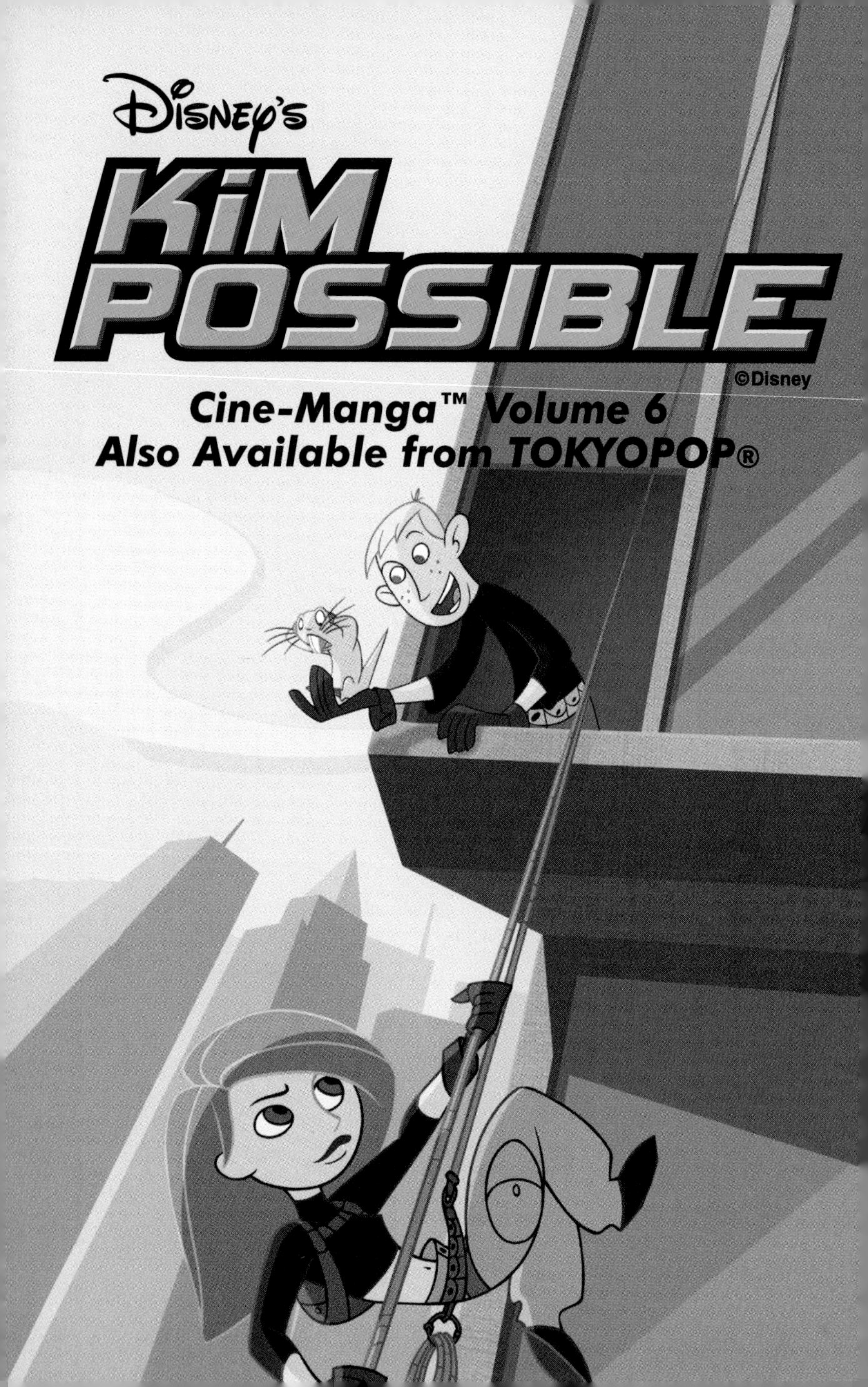
Disney's
Kim Possible
©Disney
Cine-Manga™ Volume 6
Also Available from TOKYOPOP®

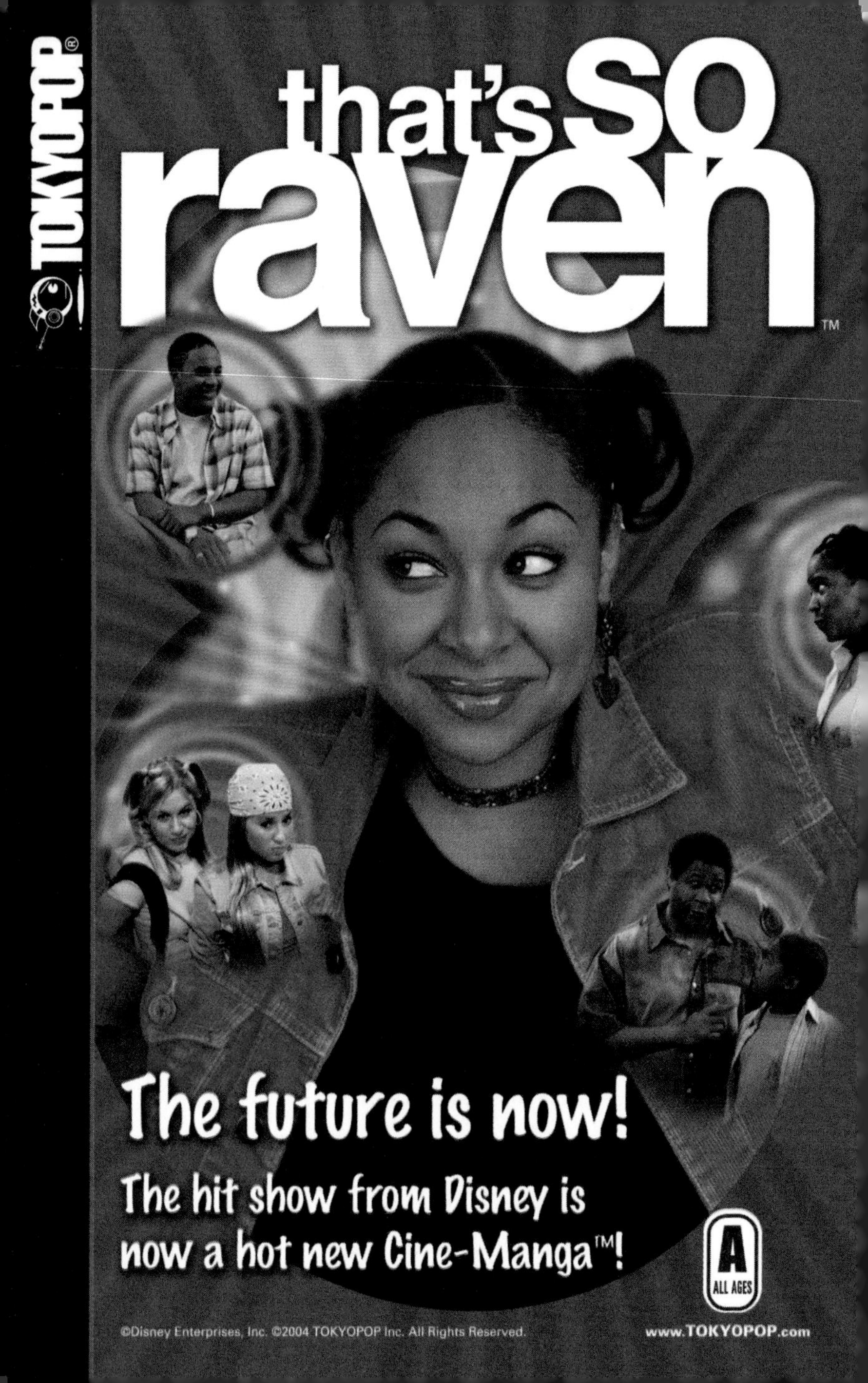
TOKYOPOP
that's so raven™
The future is now!
The hit show from Disney is now a hot new Cine-Manga™!
A ALL AGES
©Disney Enterprises, Inc. ©2004 TOKYOPOP Inc. All Rights Reserved.
www.TOKYOPOP.com

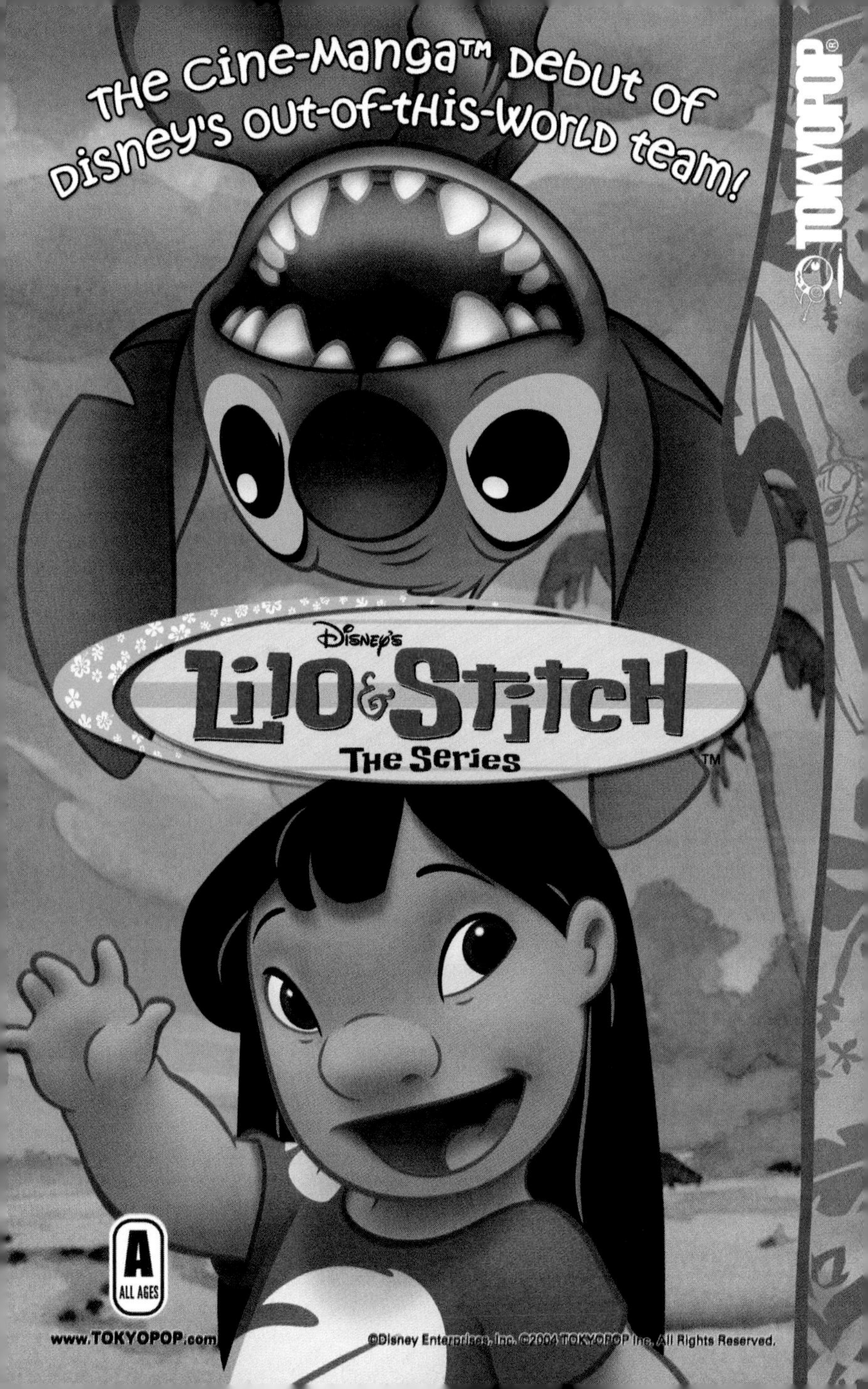

THE Cine-Manga™ DEBUT OF
Disney's OUT-OF-tHIS-WORLD team!
TOKYOPOP®
Disney's
Lilo & Stitch
The Series™
A
ALL AGES
www.TOKYOPOP.com
©Disney Enterprises, Inc. ©2004 TOKYOPOP Inc. All Rights Reserved.

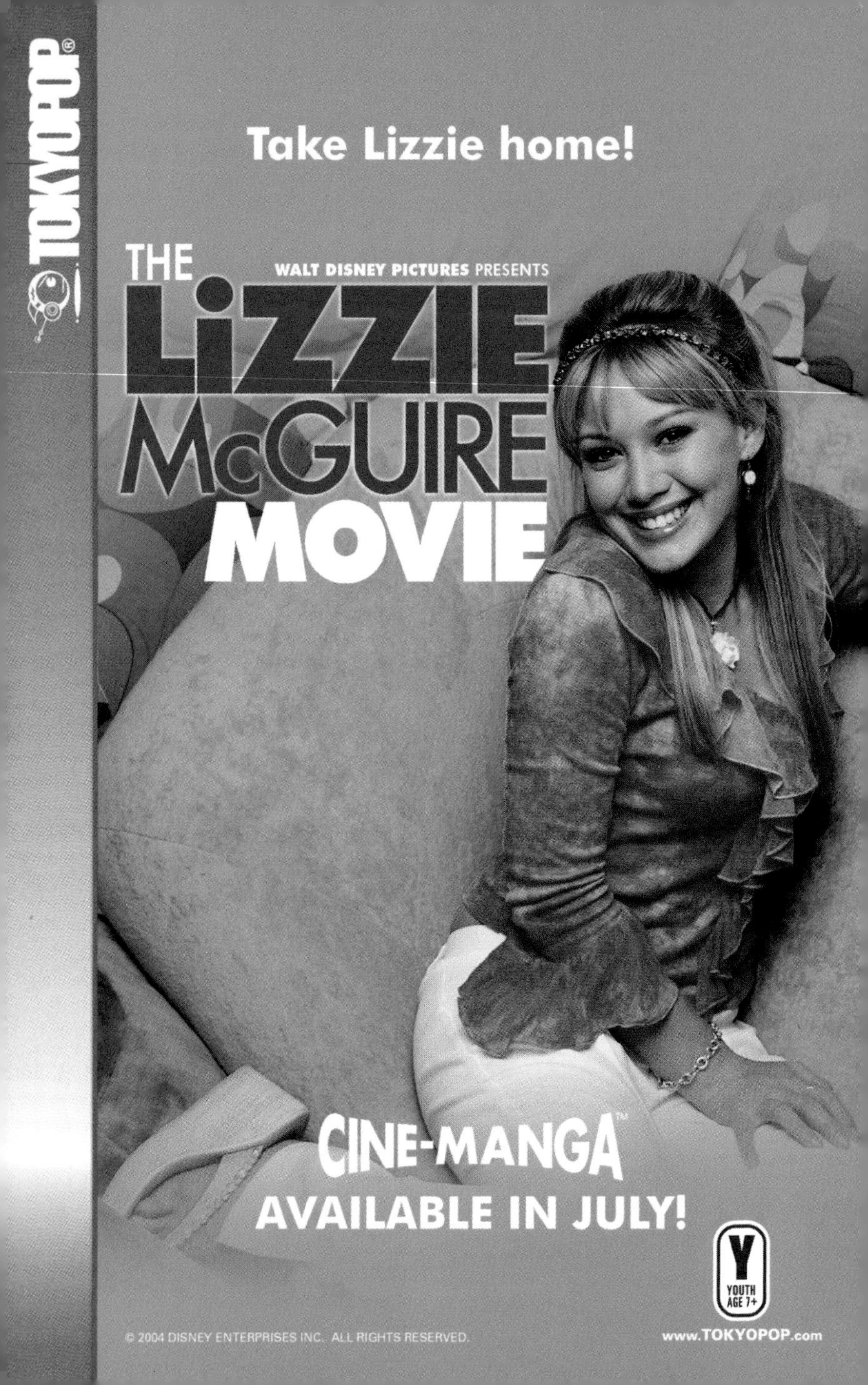
TOKYOPOP®
Take Lizzie home!
THE
WALT DISNEY PICTURES PRESENTS
LIZZIE
McGUIRE
MOVIE
CINE-MANGA™
AVAILABLE IN JULY!
Y
YOUTH AGE 7+
© 2004 DISNEY ENTERPRISES INC. ALL RIGHTS RESERVED.
www.TOKYOPOP.com